RETHINKING DEVELOPMENT

Edited by

Ndongo Samba Sylla

Published by the Rosa Luxemburg Foundation

Rosa Luxemburg Foundation
West Africa Regional Office
Dakar, Senegal
http://www.rosalux.sn

© 2013 Rosa Luxemburg Foundation

The publication of this book was made possible with funds made available from the German Federal Ministry for Economic Cooperation and Development.

ISBN-10: 1493713248
ISBN-13: 978-1493713240

CONTENTS

ACKNOWLEDGMENTS

This book is a collection of papers that were presented at a conference held in Dakar between June 26 and 28, 2012, at the Rosa Luxemburg Foundation Office for West Africa. The theme of the conference was "What changes for Africa? Which actors will carry them out?" All our partners kindly accepted our invitations to attend along with civil-society and academic actors.

We would like to thank all our partners sincerely. First, speakers Mr. Mamane S. Adamou, Dr. Okopu Aidoo, Mr. Assane Mbaye of the Alliance for Rebuilding Governance in Africa, Dr. Mor Faye, Dr. Ike Okonta, Dr. Kehinde Olayode, and Dr. Fidelis Allen. Next, discussants Mr. Boubacar Seck, Conseil des ONG d'appui au Développement (CONGAD), Senegal; Mr. Ibrahima Sène, Parti de l'Indépendance et du Travail (PIT), Senegal; Ms. Odile Faye, Association of African Women for Research and Development (AAWORD), Senegal; Dr. Tidiane Kassé, Fahamu/Pambazuka; Mr. Sam Ajufoh, Action for Community Development (ACD), Nigeria; Mr. Ken Henshaw, Social Action, Nigeria; Ms. Chrystel Lemoing, Fondation Gabriel Péri, France; Dr. Arndt Hopfmann, Rosa Luxemburg Foundation; Ms. Mary Torgbe, Trade Union Congress, Ghana; and Mr. Nouhoum Keïta, Association des Résidents et Amis de la Commune de Faléa (ARACF), Mali.

His Excellency Mansour Sy, Minister of the Civil Service, Labour, and Relations with Institutions Senegal, graced us with his presence. We would also like to thank Mr. Heinz Vietze, chairman of the Rosa Luxemburg Foundation, who insisted on attending the conference in order to take part in the discussions and to present the work of the foundation. This conference provided opportunities to discuss the multifaceted European crisis as well as the situation in Mali. We would like to thank Dr. Thomas Sablowski and Mr. Mohamed ag Akératane of Radio Kayira for enlightening us on both topics.

Finally a big thank you to all those who contributed to the success of this conference as well as the publication of this book: Ms. Kolo Diallo, Ms. Mariem Ndiaye, Ms. Clementine Thiam, Mr. Yoro Fall, Mr. Damien Sarr, and Mr. Djiby Ba. Let us not forget our translators: Ms. Carole Small Diop, Mr. David Clement Leye, Mr. Madior Diallo, Ms. Maymouna Diallo Ka, and our colleagues Dr. Bruno Sonko and Dr. Ibrahima Thiam.

Dr. Claus-Dieter König, director of the Rosa Luxemburg Foundation Office for West Africa
Dr. Ndongo Samba Sylla, researcher at the Rosa Luxemburg Foundation Office for West Africa

---

Authors' Details

Mamane Sani Adamou: General secretary of the Organization for New Democracy. Member of the board of directors of Alternatives Espaces Citoyens Niger: www.alternativeniger.org. E-mail: masaniad@yahoo.com.

Kojo Opoku Aidoo, PhD in political science. Research fellow and coordinator, History and Politics Section, Institute of African Studies, University of Ghana, Legon, Accra. His books include *Political Stability in Ghana: Since the 1992 Re-Democratization Wave*, VDM Verlag, 2008, and *Political Participation, Governance, and Neopatrimonial Rule in Africa: The Case of Ghana—1990–2000*, VDM Verlag, 2008. E-mail: aidoo77us@yahoo.com.

Fidelis Allen, PhD: Senior lecturer in the Department of Political and Administrative Studies, University of Port Harcourt, Choba, Nigeria. Author of *Implementation of Oil Related Environmental Policies in Nigeria: Government Inertia and Conflict in the Niger Delta*, Cambridge Scholars Publishing, 2012, and several articles in local and international journals and books. E-mail: allfidelis@gmail.com.

Mor Faye, PhD: Sociologist of media and communication. Researcher and lecturer at the University of Gaston Berger, Saint-Louis, Senegal. Head of the Department of Communication of the UFR Civilisations, Religions, Arts and Communication. Coordinator of the documentary movie *Master*. Director of communication and marketing, Gaston Berger University. Author of *Presse privée écrite en Afrique francophone. Enjeux démocratiques*, L'Harmattan, 2008, and coauthor of *La Charte africaine de radiodiffusion. Quel impact en Afrique de l'Ouest?* E-mail: mor.faye@ugb.edu.sn.

Ike Okonta, PhD: Coordinating fellow, New Centre for Social Research NCSR, Nigeria, a public-policy think tank that works with a wide range of civic and political groups including the Nigerian government. He has published many articles in *Project Syndicate* and the *Guardian*. Author of *When Citizens Revolt: Nigerian Elites, Big Oil and the Ogoni Struggle for Self-determination*, Africa Research & Publications, 2008, and co-author of *Where Vultures Feast: Shell, Human Rights, and Oil in the Niger Delta*, Verso, 2003. E-mail: igokonta@gmail.com.

Kehinde Olusola Olayode: **PhD** from Cambridge University, United Kingdom. Senior lecturer, Department of International Relations, Obafemi Awolowo University Ile-Ife, Osun State, Nigeria. He specialises in governance, civil society, and developmental issues in Africa. E-mail: kolayode@oauife.edu.ng.

Ndongo Samba Sylla, PhD in development economics. Programme and research manager at the West Africa Office of the Rosa Luxemburg Foundation. Author of *Redécouvrir Sankara. Martyr de la Liberté* Exchange & Dialogue, 2012, and *The Fair Trade Scandal. Marketing poverty to benefit the Rich*, translated from French by Pluto Press, 2014. His recent research work deals with the history of the word *democracy*. E-mail: n.sylla@rosalux.sn.

ACRONYMS

AD: Alliance for Democracy (political party in Nigeria)
AFRICOM: United States Africa Command
AQIM: Al-Qaïda in the Islamic Maghreb
CD: Campaign for Democracy (civil-society organisation in Nigeria)
CEDAW: Convention on the Elimination of All Forms of Discrimination Against Women
CNPC: China National Petroleum Corporation
COP: Conference of parties
CPC: Congress for Progressive Change (political party in Nigeria)
CSO: Civil-society organisations
DA: Democratic Alternative (political party in Nigeria)
ECOWAS: Economic Community of West African States
GAD: Gender and development
GDP: Gross domestic product
GEWE: Gender equality and women empowerment
ILO: International Labour Organization
IMF: International monetary fund
IYC: Ijaw Youth Council
MDG: Millennium development goals
MEND: Movement for the Emancipation of the Niger Delta
MNLA: Mouvement National de Libération de l'Azawad
MOSOP: Movement for the Survival of the Ogoni People
NADECO: National Democratic Coalition (political party in Nigeria)
NATO: North Atlantic Treaty Organization
NGO: Nongovernmental organisations
NLC: Nigeria Labour Congress
NPN: National Party of Nigeria

NRC: National Republican Convention (political party in Nigeria)
OECD: Organisation for Economic Co-operation and Development
PDP: People's Democratic Party (political party in Nigeria)
SAP: Structural adjustment programme
SDCEA: South Durban Community Environmental Alliance
SDP: Social Democratic Party (political party in Nigeria)
SNG: Save Nigeria Group (civil-society organisation in Nigeria)
TSCTP: Trans-Saharan Counter-Terrorism Partnership
TSGP: Trans-Saharan Gas Pipeline
UNDP: United Nations Development Programme
UNEP: United Nations Environment Programme
WID: Women in Development

FOREWORD

Arndt Hopfmann

If he is not to be deprived of the results obtained or to forfeit the fruits of civilisation, man is compelled to change all his traditional social forms as soon as the mode of commerce ceases to correspond to the productive forces acquired.

—Karl Marx[1]

June 2012: In those days it was impossible to prepare a conference on social and economic changes and their protagonists without being overwhelmed by two egregious events. They were like the writing on the wall, influencing practically all interventions whether they were formal deliberations on the true meaning of democracy or concerned about the lasting fragmentation of the Nigerian civil society, and they dominated the debates during the conference even more.

The first very telling incident was the presidential election in Senegal and the vibrant public protests during the time of the election campaign. Eventually, and somewhat unexpectedly, the elections went like a showpiece out of a manual on good governance but brought about almost nothing of the expected. Despite a regime change, the dreams and hopes of ordinary people about the possibility of major improvements in their lives were dashed. And honestly this was nothing more than was to be expected. "If elections under capitalism were able to bring about change, they would be completely forbidden," wrote German writer and journalist Kurt Tucholsky almost one hundred years ago. If proof were needed for the limitations of even the best-functioning multiparty system when it comes to bringing about social and economic change, Senegal could serve as a brilliant

---

1 Karl Marx in a letter written to Pavel V. Annenkov, December 28, 1846. Source: Karl Marx, *Marx Engels Collected Works* Vol 38; London, International Publishers 1975, 95

example. But the real issue goes much deeper. The more we feel we must not continue in the way we produce, consume, and live, the more we seem to be unable to do the things that are obviously necessary. And multiparty elections, with their symbolic rites and barren results, are simply infertile in this regard. But the same applies to the old concept of revolution. Civil-society activists are literally lost in the woods. This is the dilemma. "There must be some way out of here"[2]—but it is yet to be found.

If change is possible at all then it seems to be bound to the worst; this is the lesson to be learned from the events in Mali, where a coup d'etat paved the way to the occupation of Northern Mali by fundamentalist Islamic forces. The developments in Mali were the second big issue that dramatically impacted the discussions during the conference. While the multiparty system is obviously too dysfunctional to bring about meaningful and real democratic participation of the masses in order to change socioeconomic conditions for the better, the events in Mali showed the ugly face of the only existing alternative: the reinvention of the Dark Ages as superbly armed modern barbarism. But this is not yet the end of the story and not the only lesson to be learned because salvation from one beast is obviously not possible without unleashing another: the spectre of neocolonialism.

Without self-determined, people-driven movements for real democratic (i.e., participatory) social and economic change, West Africa remains trapped between two evils—the juggernaut of a growing social divide between a few incredibly rich and a multitude of abject poor, dominated by foreign powers under the guise of neoliberal globalisation, and the backslide into a highly sophisticated, allegedly religious-based but nevertheless barbaric dictatorship

Thus the search for social change and the empowerment of its protagonists is a burning but very challenging issue that our conference, held in June 2012, could not hope to solve. But it has provided some insights and some building blocks, a few of which interested readers and activists will find in this volume.

Berlin, March 2013

---

2 Bob Dylan, "All Along the Watchtower," Columbia, *John Wesley Harding*, 1967 (Released November, 1968)

INTRODUCTION

Ndongo Samba Sylla

Fifty years after independence, the need for radical structural changes on the African continent is more acute than ever. The political models that have been experimented with thus far have all reached their limits. If the single-party model proved disastrous in retrospect, the adoption of the multiparty system and the tentative walk toward representative democracy that followed are still not convincing in terms of the results achieved.

All over the continent, whatever the differences between countries in their systems of government, political power seems to have been confiscated by elites who are increasingly disconnected from the concerns of their populations. The apparent democratisation of institutions has not led to a genuine democratisation of political power. The gap between government and the governed has widened as a result of the increased disconnection between the social and economic spheres. Economic policies have been dictated more by the demands of the international capitalist system and its institutions than by the needs of Africa's peoples. Increasingly, economic policies have been decided in such ways that democratic oversight barely exists. As a result political actors have become more accountable to economic actors—i.e., to donors, foreign investors, multinationals, etc.—than they are to their own citizens.

Following the catastrophic failure of two decades of structural adjustments, Africa was immediately caught in the net of the neoliberal agenda of good governance: economic liberalisation in the areas of trade, investment, and finance; intensification of the exploitation of natural resources; and land grabbing. The result has been an increase in income for a minority and increases in capital transfers outward to the rest of the world combined with an increased marginalisation of the majority.

The continuation of such political and economic policies will inevitably undermine the future of the continent. The changes the populations have long awaited have not materialised. Unfortunately it is far from given that current political strategies will result in structural changes. Since reforms can no longer deliver change, there must be a breakaway from existing frameworks.

Finding sustainable solutions to the problems African states face has become a major challenge. This is especially the case in the context of a number of critical factors: the struggle to establish political regimes that are more inclusive and more sensitive to popular concerns; the need to build peace; the need to speed up political and economic integration of the continent; the need to implement socioeconomic policies capable of overcoming poverty; ensuring food security; creating quality jobs for a growing labour force; creating appropriate infrastructure; preventing environmental destruction; fighting against land grabbing and the depletion of natural resources; climate change; and much else besides.

According to UN forecasts, Africa will account for a quarter of the world's population by 2050. If Africa is still unable to address adequately the problems its billion inhabitants face, how will it do so when its population doubles?

The situation is made even more critical by the increasing redeployment of classic imperialism in its most hideous and least civilised form—with military invasions and regime change in several countries including Somalia, Libya, and Côte d'Ivoire. The hegemonic powers' approach has been to secure Africa's emerging markets at whatever cost. This strategy is echoed domestically by governmental efforts to improve the business environment and improve the governments' rankings in international competitiveness. As a result what is considered a breakthrough is often limited to purely scriptural economic growth—in other words a form of growth that is more visible in statistics than in the day-to-day lives of the majority, that does not create jobs and which, in many cases, is maintained by foreign investments injected primarily in natural-resource extraction.

Africa can no longer afford to waste time. Given the breadth of challenges to be overcome, there is a crucial need to adopt perspectives that are different from current approaches to development. To do this it is not enough simply to point out the shortcomings and limitations of what exists, namely neoliberalism. We need to go beyond that, to offer credible alternatives that have the capacity to prove fruitful in the long term. This is where those concerned with the future of the continent should position themselves. The brutal 2008 systemic crisis of capitalism showed that neoliberalism is unable to resolve the major economic and environmental problems facing the planet, and the time has come to envisage other models, other paradigms, and other frameworks. It is time to seize the opportunity.

Such was the conviction of the Rosa Luxemburg Foundation Office for West Africa when it organised a conference in June 2012 focusing on two main questions: What changes does Africa need? And who should be the agents of change? The objective of this meeting was to generate discussion around alternatives that would enable Africa to break out of its current deadlock. This collection is a compilation of the main contributions to the conference.

In the first chapter, Ndongo Samba Sylla argues that if we are to change things, new modes of thinking and new conceptual systems are needed. He argues that most available theories are unable to address adequately the central challenges Africa faces owing to their lack of historical specificity. He challenges the assumption that underdevelopment in Africa is caused by a democratic deficit. Democracy, he suggests, is one of the most abhorred concepts in the history of Western political thought, and he describes the semantic transformation it has undergone since the nineteenth century.

Sylla argues that systems currently described as democracies are in fact oligarchies—the rule of the few initially created to dispossess people from any political power and to secure for capital the structural basis for accumulation. He argues that "liberal democracy" is not a guarantee of economic development. Rather the insistence on the desirability of this particular political form hides the fact that countries describing themselves as champions of democracy are those where a minority rule not only over their own country but also over the world. This minority controls the majority of the wealth produced by humankind. Liberal democracy is not a solution, he argues; it is rather part of the problem. We should therefore seek to establish modes of delegating political authority that would enable greater political involvement of populations and reflect the sociological diversity of nations. A first step in this direction would consist of breaking the monopoly of political parties in the political space.

In chapter two Mamane Sani Adamou identifies four main challenges for people-centred social change: the challenge of state construction; the democratic challenge; the challenge of development; and the strategic challenge. He argues that the project seeking to establish sovereign, sustainable, peaceful, prosperous, and democratic states is seriously undermined by the deployment of the instruments of hegemonic power wielded by the United States, Europe, and China. These powers consider Africa only as a reserve of natural resources and markets to be conquered.

To illustrate this point, Adamou uses the example of the Sahelo-Saharan region, a zone shaken by a security crisis and in an endemic state of conflicts fuelled by rivalries between great powers, which often build on a comprador alliance that somehow achieves an apparent democratic legitimacy via the electoral system. According to Adamou only an alliance of popular classes can carry out a democratisation project that is synonymous with social progress and based on an autonomous, people-centred development.

Kojo Okopu Aidoo argues in chapter three that since their freedom from the shackles of colonisation, African countries have experimented with all imaginable models of development both economic and political. If these have not produced genuine development, it is because African states simply did not develop tailor-made development agendas that addressed the specificities of their countries and peoples. They resorted instead to imported paradigms based on an acceptance of the capitalist system, namely one in which African countries were locked as peripheries of the international capitalist system, being considered first and foremost as raw-material producers and exporters. Aidoo argues that development within the capitalist system is a blocked option, a strategy that is unlikely to bring development for the continent. Instead he proposes a democratic development strategy with a vision of development in which African peoples are the agents of change, both the means and end of the process of development. Development needs to be seen as a process that starts by addressing the immediate surroundings. To bear fruit this ambitious strategy requires that ordinary citizens are its architects.

In this quest for democratic development, one thing should, however, be taken for granted: no significant and genuinely democratic change can take place without the involvement and active participation of the social group that represents the demographic majority in Africa: women. This is the message Kehinde Olosula Olayode conveys in chapter four. Olayode seeks to clarify the relationship between governance, gender equality, poverty reduction, and African development. He argues these are the issues that need to be taken into account when designing policies and implementing public expenditure. To complete his argument, Olayode insists on the roles that local NGOs, development partners, and national political decision makers can play in the framework of promoting gender-sensitive governance programmes.

In addition to the question "what is to be done?" there is the question "who can do it?" What are the roles of social movements and civil society—phrases that are in need of much great analytical clarity in relation to the process of social change? There is no doubt that African social movements have often played pioneering roles in democratic advances. But do they have sufficiently strong shoulders to bring about thorough fundamental social transformations? Is it naïve to think that social movements can succeed where the politics have failed? Can we bring effective and lasting change from outside the formal public sphere?

In contrast to disproportionately optimistic rhetoric on this subject, Ike Okonta (chapter five) displays more caution. From the beginning of the 1980s, he argues, we witnessed in Nigeria what can be considered the iron law of civil-society umbrella organisations: they appeared in reaction to legitimate sociopolitical issues then gained media and popular legitimacy but ended up crushed, or tamed at best, by existing political systems. Why did Nigerian social movements lose their way in the woods? What needs to be done so they will be able to respond effectively to the legitimate democratic aspirations of the people? These are the questions Okonta raises.

For Fidelis Allen (chapter six), there is hope that social movements can manage to federate struggles beyond the myriad of daily fights by the people. Such social movements can learn from those experiences of struggle that are beginning to bear fruit. Radical social movements in favour of climate justice are emerging in many places. They are a resistance platform that can play a federating role and at the same time serve as a model for the struggles waged toward large-scale social change. On the bases of empirical materials drawn from a review of the literature, interviews with activists in Durban and the Niger Delta, and from personal observations on the activities of these activists, Allen argues that environmental issues play today, and will continue to play in the future, an important role in the emergence of local social movements that reject both reprehensible political practices perpetrated by the elites and neoliberal solutions that these elites promote in areas such as climate change, poverty, hunger, unemployment, inequities, etc. His deep-seated conviction is that the struggles taking place within this perspective can usher in alternative developmental models where oppressed classes are at the heart of policies and the organisation of production.

Based on a comparison between Senegal, Togo, and Benin, Mor Faye (chapter seven) suggests African private media played a significant role in overturning single-party regimes and in the evolution toward political pluralism. He argues that private media can be the guarantor of free democratic interplay by awakening citizens. In spite of the objective limits imposed by economic difficulties and lack of training, corruption, and the lowering of journalistic standards, Faye believes that African private media can be crucial actors for social change in Africa provided policies are better targeted toward them.

The texts compiled here are a modest contribution to the debate on people-centred anti-capitalist alternatives. Even if the analyses focus mostly on West Africa, these essays will help readers draw lessons that can be applied to the continent as a whole. This volume will have reached its objectives if it succeeds in convincing readers of the pressing need not only to think differently but to act differently in order to construct the proud and sublime Africa of which we all dream.

CHAPTER 1

CASTING DEMOCRACY ASIDE, OR DECONSTRUCTING THE DEMOCRATIC DISCOURSE? ON THE NEED TO THEORIZE AND PRACTICE POLITICS DIFFERENTLY

Ndongo Samba Sylla

Today, chaos hides behind one word: Democracy.
—François Guizot, French historian and politician

Yes, Africa needs alternatives. Yes, the recipes that have been tested for the last fifty years have all failed. (Neo)liberalism is not the solution. It is rather the problem. This is also true. What can be done, then? If Africa needs new political and economic alternatives, identifying these no doubt requires turning to new theoretical alternatives. Africans have a tendency to criticize Western models. But this critique seldom goes beyond ideology. It rarely leads to radically challenging the language of the social sciences imported from the West. The paradox is that African intellectuals seldom depart from attempting to square the circle no matter how fierce their criticism toward the West. They reject its ideology, but they keep its language and evaluation systems. Unless conceptual frameworks that reflect an African perspective are adopted, the quest for new alternatives shall remain in vain. As is often the case, the perspective for criticism tends to be African whereas that for reflection and solutions is Western.

My assumption is that most of the concepts and theories currently available when it comes to Africa are unsuited and even improper for adequate knowledge as they tend to be built according to specific parameters, based on which their relevance is generally limited when transposed into other contexts. This is what has been referred to as "the problem of historical specificity," or the need for an epistemology that is suited and sensitive to various historical configurations (Hodgson 2001). There is also the fact that the language of social sciences taught in universities often includes a subtle racialist bias, which generally reflects the perspective of power—in other words the perspective of the dominant forces.

To illustrate this point, there is no better example than the theme of democracy in Africa. Indeed an increasingly prevailing idea is that the lack or even the deficit of democracy slows down economic development on the continent. I am going to demonstrate that this approach is misguided as its proponents are not aware of the limits of the language they use. Further still, as I am going to argue, democracy is part of the problem rather than the solution. The problems of the continent, as well as the remedies that should be provided, lie elsewhere.

Acknowledgment of a Democratic Deficit in Africa

In spite of the hopes generated by the adoption of the multiparty system at the beginning of the 1990s, democracy has been faring poorly in Africa. This assessment is universally shared. No one challenges this fact. Elements that back this are so numerous, they may seem suspicious to those who generally distrust orgies of evidence. For now let us focus on the case of West Africa over the last three years.

In 2010 Côte d'Ivoire seemed to be giving a few glimmers of hope. Alassane Ouattara and the outgoing president, Laurent Gbagbo, were able to posit their identities as democrats during a relatively serene presidential debate that was widely publicised. In the end a military intervention by foreign powers was necessary to overcome the deadlock between the two candidates, each of whom had proclaimed himself president.

In Liberia the 2011 presidential elections saw outgoing president Ellen Johnson Sirleaf opposed to Winston Tubman. The latter eventually boycotted the runoff election, arguing there were frauds during the first round of voting. As a result the percentage of voters dropped from 71.6 percent to 38.6 percent. As could be expected, Ellen Johnson Sirleaf got reelected with a little more than 90 percent of votes.

In Mali, in the context of the crisis that prevailed (and still prevails) in the north of the country, an impromptu coup in March 2012 overturned the Amadou Toumani Toure regime barely a month before the scheduled date for the first round of presidential elections. Since then Mali has been struggling to return to constitutional normality, to use a well-established phrase. Although it used to be considered a model of democracy in Africa, we should point out that the number of voters in legislative and presidential elections in Mali never reached 40 percent.[1]

In Guinea-Bissau a similar scenario unfolded in the same period. Between the two rounds of the 2012 presidential election, a coup took place as a reaction to an electoral process deemed nontransparent and rigged. In Guinea, political actors have been waiting more than ten years for new legislative elections to be held.

In fact only Senegal seems to have held up well since independence. It is a rare case among African countries never to have had a coup or military rule. In March 2012 a new political changeover[2] backed by a clear poll decision put an end to Wade's attempts to remain for a third term of office. This helped to strengthen the status of Senegal as a model of democratic maturity. It is worth pointing out that the uncertainty that weighed on this election continued until the eve of the vote. The preelection context was marked by a flaring up of violence and an increasing number of demonstrations. This in fact led to several casualties and injuries.

---

1 On electoral statistics, see, for example, the Africa Elections Database website: http://africanelections.tripod. com/.

2 This word must be used with caution as a *changeover* of the political parties in power does not necessarily lead to the changes the people expect. I think this word has come to stand for the oligarchic rotation of power rather than a genuine break in terms of policy orientations.

Let us sum up then. First, numerous African countries have thus far been unable to organize free and transparent elections on a regular basis. Second, elections are often times of tension and uncertainty in most African countries. Third, elections seldom lead to structured and serene political-power transitions. Finally, countries that are supposed to be the most mature from a democratic point of view remain fragile and are generally unable to build genuine political involvement.

This reality is well known. It is reflected namely in international democracy rankings, which usually paint a bleak picture of the continent. According to the *Democracy Index*, Africa only had ten democracies in 2011 (nine considered "flawed" and only one described as "full") out of a sample of forty-four countries. According to this indicator developed by *The Economist*, the vast majority of African countries belong to the category of "authoritarian regimes" or "hybrid regimes" (Economist Intelligence Unit 2012)[3].

It is one thing to say democracy is going badly in Africa. But it is quite another to explain why this is the case. There are three main perspectives on this point. There are ethnocentric and racist theories according to which Africans, for reasons related to their habits, cultures, beliefs, etc., are incapable of establishing democratic institutions based on the model of Western countries. Somehow the problem is claimed to be a racial or cultural one. This is the perspective of those who preach from the comfortable distance of the West.

There are those who attribute this democratic deficit to a lack of leadership. African heads of state are accused of being the problem. They are not sufficiently democratic. This is why we hear about democracies without democrats. That is

---

3 This international ranking of constitutional performance is produced every year by *The Economist* (Economist Intelligence Unit, 2012). It is established on the basis of marks obtained in five areas: electoral process and pluralism; civil liberties; government operations; political participation; and political culture. The index is based on a scale of zero (worst performance) to ten (best performance). Countries with marks higher than or equal to eight are described as *full democracies*. Those with marks between six and eight are described as *flawed democracies*. Those with marks between four and six are described as *hybrid regimes*. Finally those with marks below four are described as *authoritarian regimes*. For the year 2011, out of a total of 167 countries, there were twenty-five full democracies, fifty-three flawed democracies, thirty-seven hybrid regimes, and fifty-two authoritarian regimes.

There are obviously other measures of constitutional performance that generally produce similar results for Western countries as a whole. The *Democracy Index* is used here for illustrative purposes only. In my view this measure is representative of the dominant conception of democracy among the elites nowadays. This is why it is necessary to perform a critique of the evaluation system on which it is based. This point is worth mentioning, but it is not directly relevant here.

the perspective of some African intellectuals who proclaim an authentic passion for the ideals of democracy.

There is finally the more radical perspective of researchers who find the causes of this democratic deficit in the heavy colonial heritage, in the peripheral position of the continent in the capitalist world order, and in the class relation structure.

Although my point of view is more closely aligned with the last perspective, it seems to me that most current debates on the democratic issue suffer from a fundamental flaw. They tend to be based on an obscure conceptual system that does not permit us to ascertain the whys and wherefores of this debate. In actual fact those who use the word *democracy* are most often unaware of its history, of the tensions that always prevailed between the concepts of democracy and representation, and of the premise of liberal democracy. We cannot, in my view, understand the current problems of this world if we assume Western countries are democracies or even that they are (or have been) models of democracy. This is not a value judgement or a desire to start conceptual niggles. It is a judgment that refers to history in order to make a case for its claimed objectivity.

What Democracy Hides

Democracy comes from the Greek *Demokratia*, a word that is 2,500 years old (Laniel 1995; Keane 2009, 55-56). At the beginning, in the language of political philosophy, democracy was a descriptive category referring exclusively to a *political regime*, a form of government. For instance, when a stranger came to a Greek state-city, he would often ask, "Who is the ruler here? Who makes the laws?" If this were a democracy, he would be told this: "Here all free men are equal, and all take part directly in making laws at popular assemblies."

Therefore democracy is a form of government in which sovereignty is held by the majority of free men with citizen status. It is different from a monarchy, a type of government where sovereignty is held by a single ruler, and from aristocracy, where sovereignty is held by a minority of free men. This being said, it would be wrong to assume democracy can be defined on the basis of the number criterion alone. According to Aristotle every form of government is defined in relation to the social class to which rulers belong. Thus, he continues, we can speak of a democracy only when the poor are in power. Since everywhere the poor are generally more numerous than the rich, to say that democracy is a form of government where the majority rules is, as Aristotle suggested, to inexact. "What can essentially distinguish a democracy from an oligarchy is poverty and wealth; and wherever power belongs to the rich, whether a majority or a minority, we speak of an oligarchy" (*Politics* book 3, 8.7). Plato points out that the establishment of a democratic government is generally preceded by popular revolutions during which the rich are chased out of power or forced into exile (*Republic* book 8).

Contrary to a common myth, what the word *democracy* refers to did not appear for the first time in Greece. Athens and other Greek cities did not invent democracy. The democratic system based on popular assemblies is known to have been practiced in Syria-Mesopotamia two millennia before it appeared in Athens in the sixth century BC (Keane 2009).[4] The paradox is that in the eyes of our contemporaries, Athenian democracy itself would not be perceived as democracy. Why? Because it was based on the enslavement of the majority and the exclusion of women. In ancient cities the populations of noncitizens, slaves in particular, were higher than those of citizens. Yet it is clear that for a twenty-first-century person, such realities are incompatible with the notion of democracy. This is a common mistake. Those who make it confuse the type of government with the type of society. To use Marxist terminology they confuse the *base* with the *superstructure*.

Athens was a democracy from the perspective of its type of government (its judicial/legal superstructure was that of the majority of free citizens, poor for the most part, who were thus the rulers) and not from the perspective of its type of society (the base or social relations of production). Thus Athens was a democratic government and a nondemocratic society in the sense that it was inegalitarian. This is why it is somewhat anachronistic to challenge the democratic label of the ancient republic of Athens. As long as we speak only of the type of government, Athens was indeed a democracy. We should also point out that political categories initially sought to describe only the experience of free men.

No great theoretician is known to have defended democracy in antiquity. If the most renowned and brilliant thinkers unanimously rejected democracy, the reasons given have nothing to do with the existence of slavery.

---

4 If we refer to Herodotus's *Histories*, it appears the Persians had some knowledge of the democratic system before the reforms introduced by Cleisthenes, who is described by some as the founding father of Athenian democracy (Canfora, 2004: 11).

To start with we can say that, being aristocrats for the most part, they could not be satisfied with the notion of a popular government. Democracy, in essence, is based on the assumption that the poor are the ones ruling, and those who used to be called the best or the beautiful and good should be equal to the rank and file—those who used to be called the wicked. Democracy then was seen by them as the government of the wicked. Yet for classical philosophers—the ancients—it was not natural that the wicked should govern the good. They saw democracy as a vulgar, licentious, and despotic form of government. For Plato, for example, democracy was the "worst of the good forms of government and the best of the worst," to quote his short definition summarized by Aristotle (*Politics* book 6). Plato was one of the fiercest critics of democracy, a political system that had condemned his master, Socrates, to die by drinking hemlock.

Beyond the resentment and fear caused by democracy, there were otherwise more-crucial philosophical arguments that justified its condemnation. Greek (Plato, Aristotle, and Polybius) and Roman (Cicero) philosophers distinguished between two types of government, or constitutions: the simple forms and the mixed constitutions. The simple forms are those where a single principle of government prevails. It is the case, for instance, with monarchies (principle of withholding authority), aristocracies (principle of merit), oligarchies (principle of wealth), and democracies (principle of liberty). According to these philosophers, the simple forms are unstable. Sooner or later they degenerate due to excesses in the implementation of their principles. As these are governments where one social group exerts single-handed domination, they are capable of administering only a partisan brand of justice, and therefore they will sooner or later be overturned by a revolution: monarchies turn into tyrannies, aristocracies corrupt themselves into oligarchies, and democracies become demagogies (governments where demagogues dominate) or, sometimes, anarchies or ochlocracies—the rule of the mob.[5]

Yet according to the ancient classical philosophers, a true government, the republic (*politeia*), should combine these various principles. Each social

---

5 Note that for Aristotle, democracy was an illegitimate form of government. It was the corrupted version of the political regime he named *politeia*.

class should take part in the exercise of power. Legislators wanting a just government should therefore depart from the simple forms and adopt a mixed constitution—a government based on a fair sharing of political power between the various social classes. According to Polybius if Sparta and Rome were free and long-lasting governments, contrary to Athens, it was because they belonged to the category of mixed constitutions. According to Cicero, who was inspired by Plato and Polybius, the best form of government is one that combines monarchic, aristocratic, and democratic elements.

This hatred for democracy and this rejection of simple forms was transmitted by the ancient world to the modern world. Philosophers of different eras perceived democracy as a tyrannical government that could not be fair. In fact from antiquity to the beginning of the nineteenth century, democracy remained one of the most abhorred concepts in the history of Western thought. It was linked to images of chaos and death. Evidence of this can be seen in some dictionaries of the era, wherein democracy was defined as the "despotism of the rabble," to use Voltaire's expression, and as the "subdivision of tyranny between several citizens" (Rivarol 1827). In fact while writers of the Enlightenment have often been lauded, few have commented on the extent to which they abhorred the notion of democratic government. Because they were fierce critics of absolute monarchies and their inherent values, it is generally believed that Enlightenment thinkers were proponents of democracy. This is a serious misconception. The philosophy of the Enlightenment was a radical critique of democracy. Kant, in his *Perpetual Peace*, said, for instance, "Democracy is necessarily despotism". Rousseau, the philosopher who had the most-acute popular instincts, said, "There is no government as liable to civil wars and intestine agitation than the democratic or popular" (*The Social Contract* book 3, chapter 4). Montesquieu also underscored that there can be no "political freedom" in a democracy (*The Spirit of Laws* book 11, chapter 4).

As the most-brilliant Western political theoreticians almost unanimously condemned democracy, it is not surprising the project of a democratic government was rejected by French and American revolutionaries at the end of the eighteenth century.

The Imposture of Representative Democracy

At the end of the eighteenth century and the beginning of the nineteenth, the elites (conservatives, radicals, bourgeois; intellectuals, and emerging capitalists), especially among revolutionaries, put forward four types of arguments against democracy. First of all since democracy is a system based on direct political participation of all citizens, it would be impossible for it to exist in a large state. In their eyes the system of popular assemblies, an essential feature of a democracy, could exist only in a state with a small population and surface area. In the nineteenth century, some authors felt democracy could be established only in a country with thirty thousand inhabitants at most, a figure based on the assumption that women did not have political rights (Brougham 1849, chapter 3). This was obviously a gross misrepresentation. In democracy, as underscored by Aristotle, the rule is to "govern in order to be governed in turn." [6] It has never been a matter of everyone governing at the same time.

The second argument was that democracy is a form of government of terror and one that cannot last long. Popular assemblies tend to generate factions that will sooner or later create instability and in fine result in the dissolution of government.

The third argument was that democracy is unable to resolve conflicts between different social classes. Since it would be a government that takes from the rich to give to the poor, it is a partisan government that tends to violate the rights of the small number of the good.

The last argument was that democracy is a government that prohibits the accumulation of wealth. It focuses more on equal social conditions than on the creation of wealth. Rousseau underlined, for instance, that in a democracy worthy of the name, there can be no luxury. In other words those who want to create an opulent society should envisage another type of government.

All these elements were the reason the elites were opposed to democracy. Their rhetoric often consisted of saying this was an *impracticable* system, a household word that was used frequently in their speeches every time they dealt with democracy. They considered the representative government their preferred political system.

---

6 Aristotle: Politics, Book 6 http://classics.mit.edu/Aristotle/politics.6.six.html, 350 BCE

Nowadays the idea of representation is interpreted as an institutional trick that helps preserve democratic principles in large states. This is a misinterpretation. In its origin the principle of representation was defended as being a way of curbing royal power as well as the sovereignty of the people. Initially, representative government was actually presented as an antidote to democracy. This was a system that helped avoid revolutions and protected minorities, namely the holders of capital. It used to be called *government of the able, bourgeois government, elective aristocracy, moderate aristocracy,* or *aristodemocracy*. In the United States and in England, those who would speak of representative democracy took care to distinguish it clearly from democracy, which was termed *simple* or *pure*.

The phrase *representative democracy* was used for the first time in 1777 by Alexander Hamilton,[7] one of the American founding fathers renowned for his elitism and hatred of democracy. This expression is absent from the lexicon of Enlightenment philosophers because in truth, the idea of representation is foreign to democracy. This is precisely the criticism Kant levied against democracy. As it does not admit representation, it is a government that, according to him, leads to anarchy.

The expression *representative democracy* is therefore an oxymoron, a juxtaposition of two contradictory terms. It is like speaking of a cat roaring or an elephant flying. John Adams said the expression was a "contradiction in terms" (Adams 1851, 316) and that Americans should beware of democracies, which present themselves as "liberal" (Adams, 1851, 313). As did the majority of the elite of the era, he considered democracy incompatible with freedom. It was later, in the midst of electoral jousts, that this expression was embraced and assumed in order to evade vigilant questioning by the people.

This lack of familiarity with the genesis of the concept of representative democracy explains the common mistake of considering representation as a continuation of what is mistakenly referred to as *direct democracy* (a redundant expression that makes sense only in the framework of the liberal evaluation system). Representative government is in fact based on an antidemocratic philosophy. To illustrate this let us look at two major differences that exist between democracy and representative democracy.

---

7 He used this phrase in his letter dated May 19, 1777, to Governor Morris. See Syrett (2011), Manin and Urbinati (2008).

The first is that in a democracy, magistrates are for the most part designated by a drawing of lots. Why? Because in a democracy, all citizens are equal. This means they should all exercise political power in succession. There must be a rotation of political power among citizens. Hence the resorting to drawing lots. This instrument gives shape to the philosophy of equality from the point of view of responsibilities, functions, honours, etc.

However, in a representative democracy, election is the preferred mode of designation of sovereign authority, as the most capable must be chosen. We should therefore distinguish between the elite, or political, class and the people. Whereas drawing lots enables a rotation of political power among the majority of citizens, election enables a rotation of political power among members of the elite. Election is based on the principle that political power should be held by the elites whereas drawing lots is based on the idea that each and every person should be able to take part in the management of public affairs (on these aspects, see Manin 2002).

This is the basis on which Aristotle said elections are an oligarchic instrument whereas drawing lots is a democratic institution. In his *Political Treatise*, Spinoza noted elections help us to choose "patricians," unlike drawing lots, which, according to him, is the preferred method of accessing power in democracies. In fact if we refer to the language of political philosophy that prevailed from antiquity to the beginning of the nineteenth century, the notion of democratic elections makes no sense. Only imposters and the uninitiated can use it.

The second difference is that in a democracy, the assembly of citizens is the sovereign authority. It has absolute power. It is not limited in its exercise by other sources of power. Montesquieu described democracy as a system where there is no political freedom precisely because a single authority holds absolute power in it. In contrast there is a separation of powers in a representative democracy. Political power is spread across several hands, several rulers, so it is not possible to state clearly where it lies. The advantage is that minorities can be shielded from the wrath of popular sovereignty. The inconvenient truth is that the majority can be oppressed by the rich minority who, through their influence, can keep on a leash both the people and their representatives.

In the seventeenth and eighteenth centuries, the system of separation of powers was advocated in order to safeguard commercial property against the power of kings. In the nineteenth century, as pointed out by Karl Polanyi (1944, 233), it served to protect industrial property from the democracy demanded by the people and to "separate the people from power over their economic life." In the United States, the constitution of 1787, which is a model of its kind, was established for this purpose: preventing people from disrupting a minority that is concerned with accumulating wealth.[8] To use the language of Alexander Hamilton, the goal was to "check the imprudence of democracy" by placing political power in the hands of "the rich and well born"[9] and to ensure the federal constitution is the "repository of the rights of the wealthy".[10] Madison, who is considered the father of the American Constitution, acknowledged that the main difference between former republics and the American republic is that the American people are completely devoid of political power (*Federalist 63*)—so much so that there is no constitution more antidemocratic in its spirit than the current United States Constitution,[11] where the word *democracy* does not even exist. According to Charles Beard (1986, 161), the rationale of this document is as follows: "Property interests may, through their superior weight in power and intelligence, secure advantageous legislation whenever

---

8 Nowadays those who claim to be lovers of democracy and social justice are the first to demand a separation of powers. They probably ignore that economic liberalism is also a doctrine based on the separation of powers. While the democrats of today demand a separation within the political sphere (between the executive, the legislative, and the judiciary), supporters of economic liberalism want to keep the economic sphere apart from the political sphere. As Milton Friedman, the famous "pope" of neoliberalism, wrote (1962, 21), the market system "enables economic strength to be a check to political power rather than a reinforcement." This opinion is not new. At the beginning of the nineteenth century, liberal theoreticians already considered credit as an instrument for the market to keep the states in check: "power threatens, wealth rewards; we escape power by deceiving it, to obtain the favours of wealth, it must be served; the latter must win," wrote Benjamin Constant (1819). It is thus unsurprising that socialist revolutionaries rejected the theory of separation of powers in the nineteenth century.

9 Statement made by Hamilton in June 1787 and reported by Robert Yates, *Secret Proceedings and Debates of the Convention Assembled at Philadelphia, in the Year 1787, For the Purpose of Forming the Constitution of The United States of America* (Albany 1821). See Syrett (2011).

10 Alexander Hamilton, *Constitutional Convention. Remarks on the Term of Office for Members of the Second Branch of the Legislature*, 26 June, 1787. See Syrett (2011).

11 This was demonstrated by a German revolutionary of the nineteenth century (Heinzen, 1871). The irony is that this opinion was defended in the 1920s by Walter Lippmann, an author who cannot be suspected of being a radical and who pointed out that a sincere democrat could not endorse a document such as the American Constitution (Lippmann 1922, chapter 18.3).

necessary, and they may at the same time obtain immunity from control by parliamentary majorities."

Contrary to the ideology prevailing nowadays, representative democracy has nothing in common with a democracy in the original sense of the term. Representative government is a system destined to curb the powers of the people and to promote the power of the minority over the majority. It was only given the name democracy in order to hide its true nature. In the nineteenth century, the concept of representative democracy was mostly backed by proponents of economic liberalism. This was the case with Bentham (2003) and John Stuart Mill (1991). Bentham claimed the radical democrat label and said representative democracy was the "only practicable democracy" and the only democracy that can last "beyond a day." In the United States, those who called themselves democrats were in favour of slavery. In France socialist revolutionaries such as Auguste Blanqui (2007) refused the democrat label and distanced themselves from the concept of democracy as they thought the bourgeois and the aristocrats loved these words, two social groups who avoided the use of conflicting words such as proletarian and bourgeois. Marx and Engels had used the word *democracy* in its original sense and had distanced themselves from using the word in the supposed positive construct.

To sum up, representative democracy is a system in which the oligarchic principle prevails. Capitalism is nothing other than a system that formalises the domination of the oligarchic principle via the universal commoditisation of all things. And the representative system is the political form that sanctions the authority of oligarchies by an appearance of democracy.

On Democratic Performance

To understand the problems we face nowadays and those of the African continent in particular, it is necessary to depart radically from the contemporary political discourse. Current democratic rhetoric confuses the social constitution with the political constitution, the base with the superstructure, the type of society with the type of government. When we examine the political constitutions of Western countries, it is clear they are systems with strong oligarchic biases. Strictly speaking they are not democracies as the poor and ordinary folk do not make up the political majority. Better still the functions of legislation and government tend to be allocated on the basis of the principle of wealth or party politics and not on the basis of the principle of equality (the possibility for each and every person to be able to take part in the exercise of political authority). This actually helps us better understand the following comment by John Dunn (2005, 18): "When any modern state claims to be a democracy, it necessarily misdescribes itself." When it is said that Western countries are democracies, the label may apply to their forms of society but in no way to their types of government.

It is, however, obvious that there is no society with perfect equality among its members. Most of the time, substantial inequalities exist between men and women, rich and poor, majorities and minorities, nationals and foreigners, regions, etc. This is to say the only valid use of the concept of democracy in relation to Western countries is the one that says they have higher than average democratic performances compared with others.

What is *democratic performance*? From my point of view, this concept can be envisaged as referring to two types of performances: constitutional and socio-economic. *Constitutional performance* refers to the efficiency in compliance with a given political model. Nowadays, in the framework of the dominant evaluation system, this is namely the ability of various states to maintain a good liberal democracy, a system renowned to be the least bad of all. Constitutional performance thus covers the ability to organize regular and transparent elections, the ability to guarantee private and public freedoms, and more generally the ability to apply and comply with existing constitutional provisions in force. Socioeconomic performance (or economic performance assessed from the perspective of the majority) can be envisaged as referring to improving the living conditions of populations and meeting their related needs.

As a general rule, countries that call themselves democracies mean that in comparison with others, they have higher constitutional and socioeconomic performances. Likewise, when we speak of a democratic deficit in Africa, we mean most countries on the continent have poor democratic performances. This is precisely the message of an indicator such as the *Democracy Index*.

Thus, by distinguishing between the political system and performance, the terms of the problem change. The issue is no longer one of understanding why African countries are not democracies. This issue is not especially relevant since no democracy exists in this world. The issue is rather to explain why democratic performance is so poor in Africa. To do so we must first ask ourselves about the determinants of democratic performance. What do constitutional performance and socioeconomic performance imply?

Let us return to the *Democracy Index*. Among twenty-five full democracies, sixteen are countries with low population sizes,[12] defined here as fewer than eleven million inhabitants in 2010.[13] With the exceptions of Australia, Canada, the Netherlands, and Germany, twelve of the sixteen highest-ranking countries in the *Democracy Index* are low-population countries. The total population for this group was estimated at around eighty-two million in 2010, which is an average of five million inhabitants per country. In Africa, the champions of democracy, those with the best ranking are unsurprisingly found among the smallest countries: namely Mauritius (1.3 million inhabitants), Cape Verde (500,000 inhabitants) and Botswana (two million inhabitants).[14] As we can see, a small population size is a factor that positively impacts constitutional performance.

The reason for this is simple even if it is rather counterintuitive: the main specificity of small countries is that due to their small population sizes, they have greater margins for manoeuvre and greater flexibility in terms of political organisation. For example, direct democracy may be difficult to imagine in China whereas in smaller countries, there may be greater possibilities. They can successfully accommodate any type of political regime. If monarchies and dictatorial regimes were the praised systems, then small countries would also be the highest ranked. Many small, rich Arab countries are among the bad students of democracy. Indeed a strong population increases democratic pressure. On the socioeconomic front, demands are numerous and difficult to fulfil. On the constitutional front, it is more difficult to reach a consensus.

---

12 These are Austria, Belgium, Costa Rica, the Czech Republic, Denmark, Finland, Iceland, Ireland, Luxembourg, Malta, Mauritius, New Zealand, Norway, Sweden, and Uruguay.

13 The demographic and economic data mentioned above is taken from the World Bank's Development Indicators: http://databank.worldbank.org/data/home.aspx.

14 In the *2011 Economist Index*, Mauritius was the highest-ranking African country (twenty-fourth) followed by Cape Verde (twenty-sixth), South Africa (twenty-eighth), and Botswana (thirty-third). In the *2011 Ibrahim Index* ranking, an index that measures constitutional performance for African countries only, the top three are Mauritius, Cape Verde, and Botswana. See the Mo Ibrahim Foundation (2011).

To some extent Africa is handicapped by its demographic boom when it comes to achieving a good constitutional performance. Let us return to the case of the sixteen small highest-ranked countries in the *Democracy Index*. In this group there was a population average of four million inhabitants in 1960 against an average of five million inhabitants in 2010. In contrast the average African country had a demographic size of 5.6 million in 1960. Yet fifty years later, this figure had almost quadrupled to twenty million. In an initial context of fairly high poverty, this demographic growth increased social pressure and made difficult the achievement of political consensus among people characterized by broad cultural and ethnolinguistic diversity. In a certain way, we could say African countries have for the most part gone beyond the optimal size of a good liberal democracy.

Those in favour of exporting democracy tend to underestimate the importance of the demographic factor. They believe democracy can be installed anywhere without taking the specific context into account. Can one seriously think a country such as Norway, with its five million inhabitants, can serve as a political model for a country such as China, with a population 260 times larger?

If democratic performance is facilitated by low demographic pressure, it is also conditional to the level of economic development. This is all the more so for countries with large demographic sizes. Unsurprisingly, full democracies are in a vast majority in developed countries. Indeed the twenty-five full democracies account for 55 percent of the world's GDP whereas they represent only 12 percent of the world's population. In current terms the median per capita GDP is around $43 thousand. Mauritius, Malta, Uruguay, and Costa Rica are the only non-OECD member states that are included among full democracies.

Quite obviously Western countries did not dominate the world economy by upholding human rights and believing in democratic equality. International inequalities between the West and the rest were created as part of a process that lasted five centuries. Imperialism in all its guises (colonisation, the slave trade, protectionism, etc.) as well as the domestic-level repression of workers were important ingredients of the economic development observed in the centre of the world economy. Put differently, it is because Western countries have been dominating the world for a few centuries that they are able to guarantee a degree of democratic performance for their fellow citizens. It is not adherence to democratic values that helped them achieve this level of performance, which still remains fragile. In fact as their domination becomes less strong, democratic performance will also tend to decline.

As being extremely rich is a condition for becoming a good liberal democracy, one can understand the deficit in constitutional performance in Africa. In 2010 the median per capita GDP in Africa was estimated at $743 in current terms. In other words it is fifty-eight times lower than that noted on average for full democracies. Existing political systems in Africa do not command unanimity as they are unable to deliver the socioeconomic performance their populations expect. Likewise, given the low level of economic development, they are also unable to guarantee sustainable constitutional performance even if they want to—hence the unsurprising highs and lows often seen in many African countries. Organising elections in this context can be seen as an inefficient allocation of economic resources justified by the search for the lesser evil: the need to buy a minimum of social peace.

On the Democratic Label

In light of such elements, one can understand why the dominant rhetoric on democracy today expresses the perspective of force and why this is a moral of the strongest. Indeed it is often the strongest ones that call themselves democracies, assess themselves positively, give lessons to others, and pedal representations that comfort them in their own biases. This rhetoric ought to be critiqued.

If we look closely at the political and social structure of the world system, it is clear we live in an oligarchic world. The largest part of the wealth produced by humanity is hogged by a minority of individuals who live in a minority of privileged countries. The worst is that this warring aristocracy calls itself democratic and blames the poorest nations of the world for not subscribing to the ideals of equality. On this point we can certainly say the world is walking on its head.

The ironic nature of this rhetoric is also revealed in the fact that eighteenth-century thinkers described Africa and the Americas as democracies, a label they used to describe peoples considered savage and uncivilised. In the "democracy" entry of his *Dictionnaire Philosophique [Philosophical Dictionary]*, Voltaire wrote that this type of government exists only among "backward" civilisations. With much cynicism he underlined that all that was not ravaged by colonisation remained a democratic republic among native populations of the Americas. Voltaire went as far as claiming that "much refinement" is needed to have a monarch! In other words African peoples were savages just over two centuries ago because they lived in democracies. African people are now belittled for not having democracies. Look at the contradiction!

African intellectuals often have illusions about liberal democracy. They want the benefits it may provide, but they never ask themselves if Africa has the means to cover the cost of adopting this oligarchic technology. Attempting to import democracy is an undertaking bound to fail as the privileges of empires can be enjoyed only by being an empire also. The mistake is to believe that Western countries can be models for Africa as it is really a matter of dialectical relations. The day African countries become full democracies, this will certainly no longer be the case for Western countries. Under capitalism there is no model as the strength underlying each model is not something imported. One either has it or suffers it.

Countries that are considered tokens of democracy in Africa are often empty shells. Generally speaking, Africans are not the ones defining the criteria for joining the upper levels of democracy. The Western powers and a few good students have this privilege. It is only when Western political-rating agencies give their approval that an African country can become a democracy. But as with many things when it comes to Africa, more relaxed, light, and caricatured criteria are used as a general rule when assessing democratic performance. As African countries are considered lost causes, minimalist criteria are used. As a result a generous rating is usually given to those deemed especially worthy or that seem just about to manage things.

Indeed holding a few elections labelled free and transparent is enough for a country to be considered a good student of democracy. The label democracy is therefore granted to African countries on the basis of relative constitutional performance (electoral performance and a degree of respect for human rights). Thus specific African countries will be considered democracies not because they have good constitutional performances in absolute terms but because the others are even more mediocre. Hence the disillusions that unavoidably happen in countries that take their identities as democracies too seriously.

The most recent example of such democratic illusion is Mali, a democracy plagued by corruption that collapsed like a house of cards at the first tremor (Ndiaye 2012). It is actually ironic to realize the coup of March 22, 2012, was led with the aim of "fixing" the democracy of President Amadou Toumani Toure, which was accused of being a false democracy.[15] Senegal is not left behind as it is described as one of the most vibrant and mature democracies in Africa. Yet contrary to prevailing rhetoric, this is a country where democracy did not generate an economic windfall. This is no doubt the most blatant example that constitutional democratisation does not necessarily lead to economic development. In spite of regular and transparent elections, in spite of political pluralism, in spite of power changeovers, the Senegalese are on average poorer today than they were in the 1960s (Sylla 2012).

Another oft-cited example is Botswana. This democracy has the specificity of being among the most exploited countries in the world. From 2000 to 2008, the profits transferred by multinationals ranged between a maximum of 14.7 percent of GDP and a minimum of 7.8 percent of GDP. This is a level of exploitation one would not expect from a country in which citizens really control economic decisions (Sylla 2012).

In Africa, like elsewhere, what we call democracy refers most of the time to more or less moderate oligarchies, as opposed to absolute oligarchies. Their oligarchic nature is recognized through the fact that no one challenges the notion that a select few should always rule. There are simply attempts to curb their powers by implementing constitutions. This is their moderate side. Thus the concept of democratisation often refers to nothing more than the temporary limitations imposed on oligarchic powers that, in the end, always find other means to escape democratic control. It is hence unsurprising to see that the crisis of representation is a recurring theme.

Thus it is crucial to depart from the simplification whereby more democracy, whatever we mean by it, ends up producing more economic development and in fine better living conditions for populations. In Africa, as everywhere else, the countries that have had the best economic performances have seldom been

---

15   The Junta that perpetrated the coup called itself the National Committee for Democratic Recovery and the Restoration of the State.

tokens of democracy. During the last decade, Equatorial Guinea and Angola, two oil-producing countries that benefited from the oil boom, have been the most dynamic countries from an economic point of view, with annual average growth rates of GDP per capita of 14.5 percent and 8.3 percent respectively (Sylla 2009). And yet they are described as dictatorships. In Asia we cannot say either that the Chinese giant is a token of democracy, nor Singapore or Taiwan. While South Korea became a respectable democracy at the beginning of the twenty-first century, it experienced industrialization and economic development under the rule of General Park Chung-Hee (1962–1979). Those who say economic development can be achieved through constitutional or legal tricks are either naive or trying to fool people. Reforms seeking to achieve liberal democracy are conditions that are neither necessary nor sufficient for socioeconomic performance.

Democracy and Capitalism: A Hopeless Marriage

Beyond the need to deconstruct and demystify the racialist discourse that is hidden behind the dominant democratic rhetoric, it is also important to point out this is based on hiding the power relations between countries of the centre and those of the periphery in this world system (Wallerstein 2011). This leads us to think capitalism is compatible with democracy. It is as though capitalist economic development was an outcome of the efforts made to conform to or imitate the model of liberal democracy. This is quite obviously false. What determines democratic performance is first of all the status that states have on the international scene. Institutional reforms are not sufficient to create socioeconomic performance, as conformist minds tend to argue. When a government becomes more liberal democratic domestically, it will not necessarily gain international political power. The main trick of dominant powers consists in hiding this basic truth.

Capitalism being the epitome of oligarchy, it is obvious this system is incompatible with a government that reflects the social power of the people below. As argued above, representative democracy was invented precisely because it was in line with the requirements of the capitalist system. As a form of government, it gives the power to elites and makes certain they will not be threatened by the majority. Strictly speaking a capitalist society is therefore incompatible with a democratic government. Marxists and liberals agree on this point. Indeed a sincere (neo)liberal will always argue that we must choose between freedom and equality, between capitalism and democracy (Friedman 1982, 160-161).

Capitalism is a system focusing on unlimited accumulation of wealth that is incompatible with generalised democratic performance. In this system, to create wealth, poverty must also be created. This is in the order of things.[16] Capitalism implies accumulating wealth in order to accumulate further wealth; democracy is based on the assumption of equal social conditions. On this point we can no doubt object that in Western countries, this assumption is not confirmed and that capitalism and democratic performance coexist rather smoothly as some indicators show. If this fact is undeniable, the interpretation of it is wrong. Indeed under capitalism the performance people expect is likely to materialise only in countries that enjoy "imperialistic rent" and those with "sovereign project[s]", to quote concepts by Samir Amin (Amin 2012; Dembélé 2011).

At the national level, countries that receive imperialistic rent can produce good performances from the point of view of freedoms and in relation to the standard of living they offer their citizens. But at the global level, it is impossible to produce this type of performance for all citizens of the world. At the end of the eighteenth century, the phrase *principle of preservation of opulence and misery* was used to refer to this dialectic. Freedom somewhere implies exploitation elsewhere. Economic development somewhere implies underdevelopment elsewhere. This is what we can see nowadays. The economic development of China and emerging countries translated into gradual de-industrialisation and a lingering economic crisis in countries that were until that point at the centre of world economy.

Thinking and Acting Differently

To take Africa out of this deadlock, we need to think differently. This will enable us to act differently. To start with we must realize Africa is having a later start than other regions. It is the most underdeveloped part of the globe. Chal-

---

16   According to Marx, "The 18th century, however, did not yet recognise as fully as the 19th, the identity between national wealth and the poverty of the people." See Karl Marx (1867, book 1, chapter 27).

lenges here are greater than elsewhere. We must also accept we do not have access to the options that enabled the West to develop its economy. The main colonial powers benefited from the direct and indirect dividends of imperialism for centuries. Likewise, in the case of Europe namely, they were able to reduce their demographic pressure through emigration of part of their labour force toward the Americas and the colonies. Finally, since what could be described as the ecological revolution, it has become clear that capitalist development is not sustainable in the long term. Not only does it take place at the expense of the environment but the economic development of countries at the centre and that of a power such as China can continue only if they can take over the resources of peripheral countries. Such is the verdict of ecological economics.

All this leads to the conclusion that Africa must find its own path. It will have to create its own model. To do so it is necessary to engage in a "sovereign project," as Samir Amin pointed out. This notion implies that without losing sight of the need for international solidarity between peoples, Africans somehow find their own solutions to their problems, decide their own priorities, and actually control their different resources and that their societies are organised to meet the requirements of their populations rather than those of capitalist accumulation.

If this sovereign project still has not materialised in the majority of African countries, the reason is mostly *political*. The organisation of power was designed to serve the interests of a small number of dominant powers. This is why a change in this respect requires that we think differently about *politics* and that we move out of the electoral-party power paradigm, which seems to have run out of historical usefulness.

The words *political* and *politician* are usually seen in a negative light in Africa. This is easy to explain. Clans and political parties withholding the monopoly of political power rarely manage to create the conditions for democratic performance as many expect. On the contrary representatives of the people generally tend to feed demagogy and socioeconomic inequalities instead of seeking ways to free their countries from states of geopolitical subordination. As a result people either revolt or, out of powerlessness and lassitude, give up politics to politicians and seek individual solutions, or they seek refuge in other forms of extremism. But as politics is too important to be left to politicians alone, the fight would consist in ending the disconnect between the political sphere (the government) and the social sphere (society). This should ensure that the economic sphere better meets the needs of the social sphere. In other words the goal is to reduce the gap between the leaders and the governed by trying to find systems that maximise popular involvement while granting populations actual decision-making and oversight powers on economic processes.

For a long time, people were led to believe universal suffrage was synonymous with democracy and that it is a power-delegation mechanism. This is a misrepresentation, as one cannot delegate power one does not hold. Those who cannot make laws hold no power they can delegate (Lewis 1832, 140-141). Do consumers delegate the power to produce goods and services to businesses? The answer is quite obviously no. The same applies in the case of the electoral-party politics tool. Voters can simply influence the market shares (electoral scores) of various candidates to political authority. Nowadays elections serve more to decide between oligarchies than as a genuine mode of expression of social preferences. This is confirmed by existing statistics on electoral participation in Africa.

At the root of the concept of democracy is the idea that all should and can take part in public affairs. This is the principle we need to protect and attempt to formalise. One could argue that direct democracy is impossible in a large state. We could reply it is hypocritical and misleading to pretend a minority of people counted in the hundreds can represent millions of people. The representative system is not a historical fatality that humankind cannot escape. We shall have to overcome it. Obviously all cannot govern *at the same time*. But all can be in a position, at one point or another, to *be able* to influence meaningfully the fates of the communities to which they belong.

The distance between the political class and the people could be justified in the context of great inequalities in the field of education. This break, this withholding of power by the elites, this exclusion of masses can no longer be defended. Nowadays representatives are not necessarily better educated than those they are meant to represent. In fact one could even question the special skills that would make some representatives of the people and not others. Looking at it closely, these special skills do not exist. What grants them this power is the opinion that liberal democracy is the least-bad political system, and without these representatives, only despotism would prevail. This opinion must be challenged.

What we must do is rethink the modes of choosing political authority. The first step would consist of breaking the political parties' monopolies on public affairs (*res publica*) by promoting political-delegation mechanisms that better reflect the sociological diversity of states and that are based on modes of selection that are more democratic than the electoral-money-party politics system. In a nutshell we must begin thinking about establishing political forms that will:

- Bring together grassroots communities and actively involve them in local issues
- Reduce the distance that separates central decision-making organs from the base at all levels of the political sphere
- Organise at all levels of the political sphere a rotation of political power that includes ordinary citizens to ensure political power is no longer the monopoly of a class or elite
- Quickly demote, without much cost or procedures, those who once received the mandate to act on behalf of the collective.

A solidarity sharing of political power as well as the pooling together of energies, efforts, skills, etc.—such is the way forward. Socialists in the nineteenth century fully understood that the change people desired could come only from society itself. Africa needs a large-scale and radical reform of society not constitutional amendments to a system renowned for being the least bad of the bad systems—the central argument ever offered in favour of liberal democracy.

Social movements can play central roles in this fight for social transformation provided they focus more on a radical claim to each and every person's right to govern than on the perspective of moderating the excesses of currently existing systems. They should aspire to play key roles in terms of legislation and oversight of public policies. This is our only salvation.

References

Adams, C.F. 1851. *The Works of John Adams, Second President of the United States*, volume 4. Boston: Charles C. Little and James Brown.

Amin, S. 2012. *L'implosion du capitalisme contemporain: automne du capitalisme, printemps des peuples?* Paris: Éditions Delga.

Beard, C.A. 2008. *The Republic: conversations on fundamentals*. New Brunswick: Transaction Publishers.

Beard, C.A. 1986. *An Economic Interpretation of the Constitution of the United States*. New York: The Free Press.

Bentham, J. 2003. *Plan of Parliamentary Reform: in the form of a catechism, with reasons for each article*. Boston: Adamant Media Corporation.

Blanqui, A. 2007 *Lettre à Maillard Belle-Île*, 6 juin 1852, quoted in *Auguste Blanqui. Maintenant, il faut des armes*. Paris: La Fabrique.

Brougham, H.L. 1849. *Political Philosophy. Part III: Of democracy mixed monarchy*, second edition. Covent Garden: H G Bohn.

Canfora, L. 2006. *Democracy in Europe: A History of an Ideology*. New York: Wiley-Blackwell.

Charles Louandre, ed. 1874. *Œuvres politiques de Benjamin Constant*. Paris : Charpentier et Cie Libraires-éditeurs.

Dembélé, D.M. 2011. *Samir Amin. Intellectuel organique au service de l'émancipation du Sud*. Dakar, CODESRIA.

Dunn, J. 2005. *Setting the people free. The story of democracy*. London: Atlantic Books.

Economist Intelligence Unit. 2012 "Democracy Index 2011: Democracy under Stress." http://www.eiu.com. (Accessed 11 December 2013)

Guizot, F. 1849. *De la démocratie en France*. Paris: Victor Masson Libraire.

Friedman, M. 1982. *Capitalism and Freedom*. Chicago: University of Chicago Press.

Heinzen, K. 1871 *What is real democracy? Answered by an exposition of the constitution of the United States*. Indianapolis: H. Lieber.

Hodgson, G.M. 2001. *How Economics forgot history. The problem of historical specificity in social science*. London and New York: Routledge.

Keane, J. 2009. *The Life and Death of Democracy*. New York and London: W.W. Norton & Company.

Laniel, B. 1995. *Le mot "democracy" aux États-Unis et son histoire de 1780 à 1856*. Lyon: Publications de l'Université de Saint-Etienne.

Lewis, G. C. 1832. *Remarks on the use and abuse of some political terms*. Columbia, University of Missouri Press.

Lippmann, W. 1922. *Public Opinion (Part. 6, "The image of democracy")*. New York, Harcourt, Brace and Co.

Manin, B. 2002. *The Principles of Representative Government*. Cambridge, Cambridge University Press.

Landermore H., ed. 2008. "Is representative democracy really democratic?" Accessed March 31 2008. http://www.booksandideas.net/Is-representative-democracy-really.html.

Marx, K. (1867). "Capital. A Critique of Political Economy.", vol. 1, English edition available at http://www.marxists.org. Accessed March 31 2008

Mill, J.S. 1991. *Considerations on Representative Government*. New York: Prometheus Books.

Mo Ibrahim Foundation. 2011 "Mo Ibrahim index of African Governance." http://www.moibrahimfoundation.org.

Ndiaye, I. 2012 "Les perroquets de la démocratie." Accessed March 2013. http://info-matin.info/index.php/actualite11/2533-les-perroquets-de-la-democratie.

Polanyi, K. 1944. *The Great Transformation: The Political and Economic Origins of Our Time,* Boston, *Beacon Press*, second edition.

Rivarol, A., ed. 1827. *Dictionnaire classique de la langue française*. Paris: Brunot-Labbe libraire de l'université royale, Baudoin et Frères Libraires.

Sylla, N. S. 2012. "De la démocratie en Afrique: retour sur l'exception sénégalaise," Accessed April 23 2012. http://www.pambazuka.org/fr/category/features/81600.

Sylla, N.S. 2010. *La croissance économique en Afrique (1960-2009): particularités, dynamiques et déterminants*. Unpublished manuscript.

Syrett, H.C., ed. 2011. *The Papers of Alexander Hamilton Digital Edition*. Charlottesville: University of Virginia Press, Rotunda.

Wallerstein, I. 2011. *Historical Capitalism*, London: Verso, third edition.

CHAPTER 2

THE CHALLENGE OF STATE BUILDING: REFLECTION BASED ON THE SECURITY CRISIS IN THE SAHELO-SAHARAN REGION

Mamane Sani Adamou

For the African continent, the experience of more than half a century of independence, punctuated by thirty years of interventions by international financial institutions, has proved disastrous. What Africa needs is a real change from the policies implemented so far—a change based on genuine political building that is markedly different from its colonial heritage. It is noteworthy that postcolonial states remain incapable of exercising full authority over their own territories. The inability of these states to fulfil their main sovereign functions is one of the root causes underlying the risks of destabilisation and armed conflicts in the region. Furthermore the region is particularly underadministered and mismanaged and suffers from chronic poor governance, which dangerously undermines its future and turns it into a space for constant geopolitical confrontation over control of natural resources. It appears, therefore, that this necessary political construction is handicapped by the security crisis. The latter is illustrated by the Sahelo-Saharan example.

The Sahelo-Saharan belt is developing an endemic conflict over which the various actors have little control. Destabilising and crisis-generating factors are numerous and combine according to extremely complex logics and patterns (Taje 2010). The global strategies of imperialist powers and their interventions in peripheral countries, particularly those in the Sahelo-Saharan region, should be understood through the prism of the crisis of the capitalist system. Economic expropriation, political recolonisation, and military interventionism are its main pillars.

By analysing these new international power relationships—in particular the interplay (strategic redeployments by external and internal actors) involving oil, mine, and security issues—we can highlight the challenges to be met to achieve change that will benefit the popular majorities and define the terms of the alternative. As the Sahelo-Saharan region is difficult to define other than by its fringes, we found it necessary in this analysis to privilege the so-called sphere countries (Mali, Mauritania, Niger, and Algeria) with a particular focus on Niger, due inter alia to a larger body of available data.

A New Global Configuration

Since the collapse of the USSR and the popular democracies, the new strategic world order was supposed to be characterized by relative international stability in a world of internal violence and conflict (Abdou 2008). Has the number of interstate wars decreased? This might be discussed. At any rate we remark that there are more civil wars and terrorist violence, particularly affecting civilian populations.

The East-West bipolarism and permanent security by mutual deterrence during the Cold War seems to have given way to a North-South configuration of conflicts with the emergence of new actors (armed bands, trafficking networks, associations, and multinational companies) that are juxtaposed on the states and are often beyond their control. We are truly witnessing the decline of a model of accumulation and regulation whose most striking feature was that from 1945 to 1970, the space of capital valorisation coincided with that of political management of conflicts (the nation-state). In the absence of a global space for political management of conflicts, the globalisation of accumulation leads to the collapse of the equilibriums built in the East, the West, and the South on a highly unstable world configuration in which capitalist centres exert monopolistic control in five key areas: technology, financial resources, weapons of mass destruction, communications and the media, and access to natural resources (Amin 2012; Dembélé 2011). This is of singular importance given the seriousness of the economic crisis that has been rocking the imperialist powers since 2008 and the virtual failure of the rescue plans implemented, with Greece being a case in point. Thus the pressure exerted on Southern states is brought into particularly sharp focus especially as it is part of the search for solutions to end the crisis on the part of the dominant forces.

In their frantic search for strategic raw materials, the United States, France, the European Union, and China have turned the continent into a vast tactical field where their conflicts of interests unfold on a daily basis. It goes without saying that due to its importance in terms of economic and military security, oil is a source of economic, financial, and geostrategic concern (Tchokonte 2008). Furthermore, in addition to the exploitation of resources, control over their circulation is another reason for the rivalry between the major powers. A geopolitics of pipelines is thus taking shape in order to secure strategic transport corridors: while the United States envisions the transportation of Chadian oil through the Gulf of Guinea, China is in favour of connecting the Chadian oil fields to its oil pipelines in Sudan. The European Union, for its part, shows a keen interest in the Trans-Saharan Gas Pipeline (TSGP) project, a pipeline that would supply gas from Nigeria to Europe through Niger and Algeria. Finally the Greenstream gas pipeline for supplying gas to Italy could be another alternative gas transportation channel to TSGP (Chegrouche 2010). Under that project Greenstream would start in Chad and Darfur due notably to the size of their gas reserves.

Thus the shape of the world is being changed to meet the needs of big business and the states of the North, reminiscent of the famous 1885 Berlin Conference, which resulted in the partitioning of Africa among the European powers. Today more than ever, the Southern states have to question themselves if they want to ensure they have a chance of survival.

A Niger-centred analysis of the interplay of the different actors will enable us to illustrate better the importance of the phenomenon, the risks it involves for state stability, and the democratic framework.

Analysis of the Strategies of the Players

Obviously the strategies deployed vary according to the stakeholders. Two groups of actors will be considered: external actors and local actors.

The United States of America

The USA's global strategy is embodied by two concepts: *containment* of the Soviet power (the Truman Doctrine) as the dominant strategy during the Cold War and, since the fall of the Berlin Wall, an active search for global *hegemony* (an extension of the Monroe Doctrine) by opposing both the reconstitution of the USSR and the emergence of economic and military powers that could potentially challenge its domination. In this century the USA views China as its greatest rival in the world in many areas, particularly in terms of access to natural resources such as oil and gas. Its foreign-policy strategy in West Africa seems to be dictated primarily by the oil lobby (the need for energy security), the war on terrorism (since September 11), and competition with China (Claire Woodside quoted in Obeng 2010). In 2007 US State Department advisor J. Peter Pham defined AFRICOM's strategic objective as:

> Protecting access to hydrocarbons and other strategic resources which Africa has in abundance, a task which includes ensuring against the vulnerability of these natural riches and ensuring that no other interested third parties such as China, India, Japan, or Russia obtain monopolies or preferential treatment. (Bowie 2012)

In the view of the USA, the Sahel-Sahara belt has become a lawless area, a new Afghanistan in which Al Qaida can act with impunity due to the weakness of the security forces of the states in the area. From their perspective this justifies their presence as the only one able to provide adequate logistics to reduce the threat. Obviously this forms a "diabolical couple, because wherever Al Qaida is, there goes the US army and, inversely, whenever the latter turns up somewhere, Al Qaida comes immediately." And, as always, you do not have to do very much digging to uncover "the huge interests of American companies" behind these confrontations (Malti 2008).

A review of US foreign policy actually reveals "a foreign policy strategy focusing above all on the militarization of Africa" (Claire Woodside quoted in Obeng 2010). To that end the Pan-Sahel initiative, a programme aimed at equipping at least a 150-man company in every partner state (Mali, Niger, Chad, and Mauritania), was launched in 2002. In 2005 the United States established the Trans-Sahara Counter-Terrorism Partnership (TSCTP), which replaced the Pan-Sahel initiative and which, in addition to the four countries mentioned above, also includes Morocco, Algeria, Tunisia, Burkina Faso, and Senegal. Its goal is to prevent terrorist groups from recruiting and training combatants and having sanctuaries in the region (Plagnol and Loncle 2012). But the most important aspect of US military engagement is the "regular conduct of large-scale exercises grouping American and African forces (mainly TSCTP partners) and those of certain NATO countries" known as the "Flintlocks" (Tisseron 2011). We can therefore understand Washington's interest in Niger even though its oil companies are not involved in oil exploitation, and it has shown no direct interest in uranium mining.

The People's Republic of China

Since 1995 the Chinese government has been conducting an overall international energy policy aimed at minimizing its dependence on Middle Eastern oil. China is also shaking up the development agenda and redefining geostrategic balances by imposing itself as one of the major trading partners, aid providers, and investors on the continent, particularly south of the Sahara (Alternative Sud 2011). The African continent offers real opportunities for at least three aspects of its foreign policy (Tchokonte 2008): maintaining a reservoir of votes at the United Nations, procurement of natural resources and offering new markets to its economy; and isolating Taiwan.

One of China's very subtle penetration strategies consists of offering to build refineries for local production. Thus all licenses held by Canada's ENCANA in Chad and the American company Exxon's Agadem license in Niger were taken over by CNPC (China National Petroleum Corporation) through promises to build refineries capable of producing 20,000 and 30,000 barrels per day in Niger and Chad respectively.

The approaches used vary according to the context and the country, ranging from major investments in infrastructure to supplying military materials and
diplomatic and financial support. In the Sahelo-Saharan region, China plans to
link its oil production to the Sudan gas pipeline. These opportunities were seized
by the state of Niger, which, beginning in 2007, engaged in a tug-of-war with
France (by breaking the quasi monopoly of AREVA on uranium mining) and the
United States (by deciding to supply uranium to Teheran).

France

In a highly instructive publication funded by the French Ministry of Defence,
Niagalé Bagayoko-Penone, a French woman of African origin, provides a very
interesting insight into the different strategies France and the United States
deploy in West Africa. The author states:

> France's political and diplomatic posture in West Africa is
> articulated around three main axes: (i) preservation of special
> ties with the Francophone countries in the Sub-region; (ii)
> covert action against Nigeria's influence in the area; (iii) control
> over multilateral economic and security mechanisms put in
> place in the late 1970s. (Bagayoko-Penone 2004)

Cooperation with the Sahelian states in the area of security is under the pur-
view of a Security and Defence Cooperation Directorate (Direction de la Coo-
pération de Sécurité et de Défense—DCSD) of the Ministry of Foreign Affairs.
The mechanism established includes regionally oriented national schools (École
Nationales à Vocation Régionale, or ENVR) and a Priority Solidarity Fund (Fonds
de Solidarité Prioritaire, or FSP) to fund capacity-building projects for high-level
security and justice-department employees. While globally effective this strategy
of perpetuating the colonial pact has been frustrated more than once.

In Mali as early as 1961, President Modibo Keïta denounced the military
cooperation agreements signed in Paris on July 22, 1960 and requested the evacu-
ation of the French military bases in Bamako, Gao, Kidal, and Tessalit. In Niger
in 1974, President Diori's regime engaged in a tug-of-war with COGEMA (the

forerunner of the nuclear giant AREVA) over the reassessment of the price of uranium, which culminated in the coup d'état of April 15, 1974. Subsequently Niger
was faced with two Tuareg armed rebellions in the North precisely at two crucial
moments in its history: the first occurred during a national conference featuring
rhetoric against French imperialism that was not to the liking of Paris; the second
took place in 2007, when the president of the Fifth Republic, Tandja Mamadou,
embarked on a policy of diversification of the country's mining partners.

AREVA's quasi-monopolistic position was threatened by the granting of
numerous mining titles to countries such as China. The chill in relations between
Paris and Niamey was visible in the consecutive postponement of the signing of the
convention granting AREVA the Imouraren megadeposit (a one-billion euro investment and five thousand tonnes of uranium per year). The French group needed to
ensure long-term fuel supplies to the buyers of its nuclear power stations. Having
fully appreciated what was at stake, Mamadou Tandja asked for 40 percent of the
company's capital (whereas AREVA was offering 33 percent), nearly 15 percent
of the yellow cake, and the group's commitment to constructing a railway line to
facilitate the transfer of the precious metal via the port of Cotonou in Benin (*Lettre
du Continent* 2008). With the coup of February 18, 2010, France backtracked on
its commitments: no railway line; the opening of the Imouraren mine scheduled
for 2012 was postponed indefinitely; AREVA's shares in the mine operation were
transferred to other states without consulting Niger; etc.

In contrast Chinese companies apparently had no problems with the Tandja
regime even though they lost Imouraren. A mining convention was signed on
July 14, 2006, to operate the Azelik deposit; the mining company SOMINA
SA was established on June 5, 2007, and the mining license was granted on
November 8, 2008. Niger (SOPAMIN) owns 33 percent of the shares while two
Chinese companies own a total 62 percent of the capital. The planned investments, including the construction of a thermal power plant, are worth 154.5
billion CFA, and an estimated 425 jobs will be created[1]. Niger will pay its share
through a commercial loan from Eximbank.

It may come as a surprise that the government of Niger simply maintained
the same conditions when signing conventions with China, without really taking

---

1 Fact sheets of the Directorate of Hydrocarbons, Ministry of Mines and Energy of Niger.

advantage of the competition. However, since the recent signing of $3.5 billion worth of contracts between China and France for the delivery of nuclear fuels (twenty thousand tonnes over ten years) and the transfer—without consulting Niger—of 10 percent of its shares in Imouraren (2.5 billion euros) to Peking, a new phase began in the game of the great powers (Granvaud 2012). Thus, during Chinese president Hu Jintao's state visit to France, Paris and Peking agreed to "develop [their nuclear partnership] across the spectrum upstream, i.e. in mining, and downstream, i.e. reprocessing." For its part the French nuclear group said it was "ready to open up to a Chinese partner in one of the mines in which it held a majority share" in Niger (Imouraren). As for the reprocessing of nuclear wastes, the French and Chinese partners decided to study "the conditions under which [they could arrive at] a contract for the construction of a reprocessing and mixed oxide (MOX) making plant in China" (AFP/Jeune Afrique 2010).

The European Union (EU)

Relations between Europe and Africa are three-pronged. Some European Union member states maintain bilateral relations with their former colonies; development-cooperation or trade-cooperation agreements have been signed by the EU and African governments; and finally the more-recent EPAs (economic partnership agreements) have enshrined relations between the Union and African regional and subregional organizations. Examining European policy in Africa comes down to distinguishing between these different levels, which overlap or reinforce each other in the field (Nkundabagenzi 2005). Direct management of African affairs at the European supranational level was made possible by the adoption of the Maastricht Treaty; enacted in 1993 it paved the way for the emergence of the Common Foreign and Security Policy (CFSP) and the European Security and Defence Policy (ESDP), which offers Europe autonomy of action in the military handling of crises. It allows the European Union to use military or civilian means to prevent conflicts and manage crises on the African continent.

The strategy defined for that purpose, more commonly known as the Sahel Strategy, is aimed at helping the region's countries through four strategic axes: development, good governance, and resolution of internal conflicts; policy and diplomacy; security and the rule of law; and preventing and combating violent extremism and radicalization (Plagnol and Loncle, 2008). Despite repeated claims of a will to reform cooperation with the continent and a new architecture put in place to that effect, we must acknowledged that the EU continues to reproduce the forms of dependence and the international division of labour it inherited from the colonial period.

Compared to the external actors (states and their transnational corporations), the local actors appear to be powerless at first glance. The reality, however, is far more complex.

African Governments

Most African governments have no global strategies. Weakened by decades of implementation of austerity policies, most are obliged to accept the logic of foreign powers, especially France, that they seek to use to strengthen their power. Their rentier ruling classes do not develop national and regional projects with the notable exceptions of Algeria and Libya under Gaddafi. As they accumulate capital from mining or oil income, development aid, and trafficking, their management of the state is necessarily based on corruption, clientelism, and often ethnicism. This poor governance heightens inequalities, undermines the social fabric, increases dependency, and reduces the expression of democracy to an electoral sham.

However, in this respect we should distinguish states like Algeria and Libya (prior to its destruction by NATO forces), whose socioeconomic achievements are impressive,[2] from countries like Mauritania, Mali, Niger, and Chad, which combine all the worst human-development indicators. The most-relevant actors of the group, Algeria and Libya, are of comparable economic sizes and are major oil producers.

Algeria seems to be positioning itself as a transit country in the Trans-Saharan Gas Pipeline (TSGP) project. It is also a facilitator or mediator in conflicts between the governments of Mali and Niger and their Tuareg communities. Algeria carried out joint exercises with the Malian army shortly before the new rebellion started and hosts the headquarters of the Joint Military Staff Committee (CEMOC) in charge of coordinating the state security operations of Mali, Mauritania, Niger, and Algeria. Gaddafi's geopolitical projects focused on

---

2 According to the UNDP ranking of 2011, Libya topped the human-development index in the African continent.

the whole Saharan region and were aimed at creating the United States of the Sahara, building on an ambition dating back to Senoussi in the nineteenth century (Lacoste 2011). This involvement in the trans-Saharan game took the form of mediation between Niger and the Tuareg rebels, Chad and its politico-military movements, and Sudan and its Darfur rebels. Libya's trans-Saharan and African role was reinforced by a policy of assistance targeting both states and grassroots communities through economic projects. Finally Libya spearheaded the establishment of the Community of Sahelo-Saharan States (CEN-SAD).

ECOWAS

The ECOWAS region interlocks with the Sahelian region although only partially for some of its member countries. These two partly superimposed ecological and geopolitical spaces share similar security and development issues. Yet it goes without saying that security is actually a twofold issue combining governance and development. This integration framework, established in 1975 following the call for new international order to achieve collective self-reliance and integration through a single market structured around a regional economic and monetary union, has progressively become a bridge structure for Western powers and a tool in the hands of the heads of state. ECOWAS's position during those last few years was indicative of its submission to foreign interests.

The current focus on the return to constitutional order in Bamako even though the government of Mali exists on only one-third of its territory, is demonstrative of the tremendous fear of virtually all ECOWAS heads of state of destabilisation of their regimes. The fact that the economic community blocked military equipment destined for Mali in the ports of Dakar and Conakry clearly reveals its "willingness to set aside the central government of Mali in favour of an advanced autonomy system in which the Northern regions' management would be largely entrusted to leaders of the MNLA pro-independence movement" (Allafrica.com 2012). Given that the movement has been virtually defeated and that its leaders are being extirpated from the Malian territory, ECOWAS's strategy appears to be a crude attempt at endorsing the carving up of Mali with a view to rebuilding the French Sahara, riding roughshod over the hallowed principle of the inviolability of borders.

Armed Movements (Tuareg Rebellions and Islamist Movements)

The Tuareg rebellions appear as both indicative of the failure of national construction in Sahelian states and a privileged means by which local elites harness income from the state, thereby becoming genuine political entrepreneurs. It is significant in this respect that the different rebellions pay little heed to internal cleavages or to the slave relationships that continue to prevail in their community.

With regard to the jihadist movements, we must draw on history to understand their current dynamics and determine the extent to which they demonstrate change or relative continuity with the past of a region that has experienced theocratic states, jihads, and political constructions that have sometimes taken violent forms. Indeed the history of Central and Western Sudan has been marked by armed violence and conquests but also resistance. The emergences of the great empires and kingdoms (Ghana, Mali, Gao, Kebbi, Sokoto, Ayar, Katséna, Kano, etc.) were accompanied by wars of political or religious expansion (such as the jihad carried out by El Hadj Umar and Osman Dan Fodio) and resistance as far back as the precolonial period. But the jihads of that time were different in that their motivations lay within the areas in question even though their perspectives transcended the frontiers. Furthermore they involved non-Salafist Islam (Diallo 2011). At the height of the Sokoto Emirate, the Commander of the Faithful recognized animist enclaves such as the village of Massalata near Birnin Konni in the Republic of Niger.

Networks Trafficking in Arms, Drugs, and Persons

Relations between regional trade networks and states, loci of accumulation par excellence, raise the issue of commercial income (*Hérodote* 2011). Traders and businessmen meet with political authorities to divvy up border revenue. Operators and protectors therefore share a common interest. While the latter intervene to impose their political and financial objectives on the former, the former attempt to embrace and transcend them with a view to maximizing their accumulation. "According to a study by the University of the Andes in Bogotá, Colombia, published on June 2, 2012, by the British newspaper *The Guardian*, claimed that drug trade chiefly enriched American banks, with 97.6% of their proceeds. Only 2.4% remained in Colombia" (Ndiaye 2012). Trafficking is really an expression of the financialised capitalist economy and a sign of the collapse of local states.

Regardless of the level considered, from the lowliest smugglers to major drug traffickers, corruption seems all pervasive in the Sahelo-Saharan region and greases the wheels of business. It exists in the area of migration where government officials responsible for controlling mobility (police, customs, and even military) turn a profit on it. Trafficking in arms, particularly light weapons, and cigarettes fit the same analysis. Thus whether the focus is on illicit Saharan and trans-Saharan trade, trafficking related to the criminal economy, migratory movements, or the exploitation of oil and mineral resources, the same issue—channelling revenue—seems to be at stake although the means and strategies used may differ widely.

What Changes?

The potential for change in the Sahelo-Saharan region is beset by various types of challenges reflecting the close ties between security, governance, and development.

The Democratic Challenge

The strategies of the great powers are indeed major impediments to the democratization of the continent. A review of Western and Chinese strategies seems to suggest the former is more favourable to democracy as the Western states make it a condition of aid and regularly finance our electoral processes. In contrast the lack of political conditionality in the relationships with Peking, and China's support for certain regimes that are enemies of the West (Sudan, Zimbabwe, Guinea, etc.), tend to substantiate the theory that China is favourable to authoritarian regimes.

However, the reality is much more complex. Indeed when their strategic interests are at stake, imperialist powers do not hesitate to sully their professions of faith by supporting rigged elections, covering up serious human-rights violations, or simply upholding sham democracies. After all real democratization of African states, conceived of as the political emancipation of African people, involving economic and social development for the benefit of popular majorities could be very dangerous for the achievement of the Western powers' geostrategic goals.

The model of liberal representative democracy developed in the late eighteenth century is essentially a mechanism for the transfer of power from the people to a specialized body. In a time of strong popular and social struggles, it effectively made it possible to guarantee numerous rights and freedoms. Likewise when the socialist camp, the labour movement, and the national liberation movement were powerful, this model actually guaranteed a certain amount of social progress. To this day the institutional and political practices that profess to adhere to democratic principles follow from the triumph and continuity of this concept. This induces passivity in citizens. Furthermore it leads necessarily to "an idea that democracy cannot exist if there is untimely involvement by citizens" (Zarka 2012).

In the light of the current hegemony of financial capital over productive forces and human beings, "power is increasingly shifting away from citizens, and representative democracy has become a means to absorb the grass-roots movement and to confine the notion of realism in a previously defined space" (Zarka 2012). The collapse of the Soviet bloc, the weakening of the labour movement, and the crisis of the developmental model in the South, combined with this hegemony, have led to the questioning of social rights and benefits worldwide and to the dictatorship of the market. In African states the democratic process quickly entered into crisis. The democratic game has become a penny-ante[3] exercise reduced to the rituals of elections that are rarely transparent and whose winners are almost always the most prominent candidates in the international community.

Income from oil and mining has also thwarted democratic progress in the Sahelo-Saharan space by discouraging internal political-consensus building. Thus exclusive control over access to oil revenues by the military hierarchy in Algeria has been a long-standing obstacle to the need to open up the political system. Similarly President Tandja's bid to stay in power after his second term would have been unimaginable without the substantial bonuses stemming from the signing of contracts with CNPC. The option to use force to eradicate the armed rebellion of the Niger Movement for Justice (the Mouvement des Nigériens pour la Justice, or MNJ) in 2007 would hardly have been conceivable either without the considerable military and financial resources the Chinese government made

---

3 A poker game in which the highest bet is limited to a penny or another small sum.

available to Tandja's regime. Oil revenue also accounts for both the longevity of Deby's regime in Chad and the difficulty of implementing a democratization process in the management of public affairs, where assassinations and disappearances of political opponents punctuate every electoral process.

The Challenge of State Building

The fragility of the Sahelian states is linked with issues of institutional and sociopolitical capacity and/or stability. In some instances it is fed by a governance crisis related to a corrosion of legitimacy; it is rooted in the challenges of nation building, in which the state apparatus has often been privileged to the detriment of nation building. A phenomenon that is indicative of the failure of the postcolonial state is the recurrence of identity-based and centrifugal rebellions. Three sets of explanations have been identified to account for it (Saidou 2009).

The Tuareg rebellion is firstly analysed as the consequence of a deliberate policy of political and economic marginalization of the Tuareg, inaugurated by France during the colonial period and strengthened by the postcolonial state (Dayak 1992; Claudot-Hawad 1992). A second perspective emphasizes that the postcolonial state's public policies in pastoralist areas have caused a crisis in nomadism; under this view the rebellion is a brutal expression of the divide between a rational modern state with Jacobin tendencies and the logic of a nomadic community that had no concept of state borders (Bourgeot 1990 and 1995). The third approach postulates that the rebellion stems from the state's total lack of strategic vision and a widespread governance crisis. The economic marginalization of the north of Niger was merely a reflection of the neocolonial nature of the postcolonial state, which was still playing the role it had been assigned by the colonial system (Hamani 2007). In other words the conflict in the North reflected the inability of the political elites in Niger to break from the structural imbalances between the different regions introduced by the French colonial system.

These explanations show there are deep, endogenous reasons for the recurrent crises in the Sahelo-Saharan belt. These causes are deeply tied to the management of the postcolonial state, question the experience of edification of the nation-state, and bring the national question back to the fore. In the geopolitical and strategic context described above, it should be borne in mind that identity crises are largely sparked by Western powers and nurtured by local political elites. The fact is that behind the identity and ethnic crises lurk power issues that in turn hide economic interests.

The Challenge of Development

For development to fulfil its role as a process of "collective achievement forming the essential framework for individual fulfilment," it must meet three criteria (Houtart 2003):

- It must be ecologically sustainable—that is to say environment friendly. In this respect it must break with the productivist logic of capitalism, whose ecological disasters threaten the very survival of the planet.
- It must meet the needs of all peoples and all social groups and not be subordinated to the imperatives of maximum profit seeking.
- It must promote the fulfilment of all human beings. The creation of wealth should by no means lead to the social and psychological crushing of individuals. (Houtart 2003)

Development must be put back into the context of the social relations produced by capitalism. This will allow us to measure the scope of the obstacles we must remove to make it possible. These obstacles are first and foremost macroeconomic: unequal exchange, debt, financial speculation, etc. As the goal of development is change and no longer mere adaptation, its achievement involves a questioning of international power relations. We cannot reduce development to programmes of poverty alleviation, microcredit, and humanitarian action.

The Strategic Challenge

Among the reasons that can be invoked to justify the relative ease of the current deployment of the major powers on the continent, particularly in the Sahelo-Saharan region, the prevalence of strategic weakness and the leadership's political and technological inability to control and exploit natural resources impose themselves on any analyst.

The lack of a strategic and forward-looking political vision, understood as a lack of autonomy in the definition of political goals and the management of public affairs, seems closely linked to the distinctive extraversion of the post-colonial states. It is easy to note that in the issue of terrorism, for example, the states of Mali and Niger are far from being significant targets for Islamist groups. However, their leaders, particularly those of Niger, focus on belligerent anti-jihad rhetoric every time they speak in public. In Niger this has led to a chill in relations with Algeria (*Lettre du Continent* 2012). The fact is these leaders are merely relaying the discourse of the former colonial power. They consider political Islam a danger that could justify a priority focus on the parts of their states, following in the footsteps of Mauritania, which chose to make the fight against terrorism under the oversight of Paris a top national priority, thereby compromising its rapprochement with Algeria.

This also affords opportunities to local groups and networks that can align their strategies with those of the state, further weakening the latter. It seems as though the lack of strategic vision and the extreme vulnerability of the political elite have enabled the external actors (transnational companies and northern states) to transform the national space according to their interests, thus becoming key local actors.

It is therefore urgent to move toward another type of political construction—to build a new society capable of meeting the challenges referred to above. For this to be achieved, certain prerequisites must be met in terms of strategies.

What Strategies?

For change to be achieved, a set of capacities is required. I suggest the following:

- There is a need to develop a global, integrated, and inclusive approach to strategy and policies aimed at meeting the challenges of insecurity fed by the development gap (Diallo 2011). In this framework a genuine transformation of the ineffective and costly governance of security systems must be supported so we can meet security challenges. In order to ensure the effective linking of security to development, institutional actors will have to: (i) ensure the *consistency* of strategies; (ii) build *complementarity* (of interests and means); and (iii) implement continuous and sustained *coordination* of actions.

- There needs to be a move toward democratic political construction. At this point the crucial question arises of political construction that can meet both democratization and development challenges. The democracy in question is not just the essential condition for development worthy of the name, that is to say economic, social, political, and cultural development for all lower classes. It should not represent a technical solution for addressing the issue of accession to power. "It is also an objective in itself, the very expression of the fundamental concept of emancipation of human beings, individually and collectively, in society" (Amin 2012).

  o This means we must seek active civic involvement of the masses throughout the process. The idea that citizens are unable to grasp the complexity of the problems of modern society and therefore to understand key political issues is simply unacceptable. The focus on civil-society participation (despite the ambiguity of the expression) in shaping societies "can be a useful positive method—a starting point—for posing the question of democracy in its entirety" (Amin 2012). It is the formal recognition of the fact that societies cannot be reduced to states and that the linkages established by globalisation should not be limited to inter-national relations (between states). All the requirements constituting a democracy at the service of the working classes, a democracy tied to social progress, are now called into question by global financial capitalism, its oligarchies, and its local agents.

  o At the same time, the question of building states that can reconcile and organize symbiosis between several communities as well as regional integration that serves the establishment of new international relations forcefully confronts us. The political and geographic configurations created by the colonial powers for the exclusive benefit of metropolitan economies cannot be maintained even after some window dressing. Real renewal is required. The first step toward such reconstruction is to break away from the ideology and practices of the neocolonial state. This means building a state that is accountable to people and their representatives and establishing public institutions that are able to promote development.

- We need to develop a preventive approach addressing the underlying and structural causes generating the vulnerabilities that increase risks in the face of threats. This would include:

  o Developing a culture of conflict prevention and peace building after conflicts.

  o Supporting the operational and sustainable implementation of preventive strategies aimed at youth. Act on the social roots of political violence and terrorism.

  o Promoting human rights and combating discrimination.

  o Promoting democratic governance.

  o Encouraging cultural pluralism and intercultural dialogue.

  o Convincing states and supranational institutions (ECOWAS and the African Union) to operationalise regional governance instruments that preventively address the root causes of conflict. The transnational nature of the threat should justify granting high priority to regional and international cooperation. The prerequisite for this is a consensus on the analysis and assessment of the threat in view of gradual pooling and sharing of capabilities. For that purpose social and citizens' movements must play stronger roles.

- There is a need for identifying the political and social forces that can bring about the desired changes. Doing so is an important political dimension of change. Indeed the class nature of change is a fundamental aspect that needs to be examined. In our analysis of the actors and their strategies, we should distinguish between local actors who are obstacles to the desired change and those who have objective interests in it.

Which Actors Can Bring About Change?

The Ruling Classes and Their Institutions

Social change with a view to liberation from imperialist domination cannot be designed by the rentier ruling classes of the present states. A leadership embodied by a rentier elite with very little confidence in the autonomous development capacities of their own countries would certainly be the partner of choice for the major powers and their transnational companies. The conflicts that arise between them and the imperialist powers are rarely over issues that are important for the people. To be convinced of this, one needs only to observe their attitudes in the Ivorian crisis, during NATO's attack on Libya, and recently during the occupation of Northern Mali by armed movements (MNLA, Ansar Dine, and AQIM). These forces form a comprador alliance. They are firmly grounded on a marginalized integration in submission to neoliberal globalisation.

As for the integration institutions, it is important to face the fact that in the present context, the African Union and ECOWAS are not the appropriate actors to launch an initiative that is not a prolongation of the desiderata of the European Union but "rather an experience that would address the root causes of conflicts, is beneficial to the populations, can be measured by their representatives and owned by internal actors" (Diallo 2011). Instead these institutions share one philosophy: to confine African states as auxiliaries to Western powers in the fight against terrorism, which essentially targets European nationals, migrations, and drug trafficking to Europe.

The Tuareg Rebellions

Identity-based movements such as the Tuareg rebellion fail to challenge the West's strategic interests and therefore are subject to potential manipulation by global geopolitical structures; thus they cannot achieve the desired change. The rebellion in Niger is perceived as the manipulation of Tuareg elites supported by France to defend the colonial pact that seemed to be threatened in the early 1990s by the emergence onto the political stage of forces viewed as anti-French. In this analytical grid, the Tuareg issue is seen as the product of the instrumentalisation of cultural identities for personal interests and French imperialism (Salifou 1993).

It is indeed remarkable that the different Tuareg rebellions have never focused on emancipating the *akli*, or slaves. As shown above, the dominant aristocracies' concern is to use armed struggle as a means of participation in rent seeking through better positioning in the state apparatus. That is why these movements have never threatened the interests of French imperialism. In Niger rebellions have occurred precisely every time the country had to face key issues involving its future: during the National Conference in 1991 and during the diversification of partners in extractive industries and reorientation of Niger's diplomatic map in 2007. The same could be said for Mali.

Political Islamism

Jihadist movements seem to have a more global perspective than rebellions. They do not demand independence for any portion of a national territory, and they are developing an anti-Western rhetoric (particularly anti-French) that, despite the brutality of their methods and their hostility toward women, has a certain attraction for the masses that are marginalized and disempowered by the devastating effects of neocolonial capitalism. However, their connivance with the United States and the considerable funding they receive from the Gulf countries (Qatar, Kuwait, and Saudi Arabia) cast doubt on the democratic or reformist nature of their project. Moreover they appear to have strong ties with various trafficking networks. In addition, at the programming level, they propose no credible alternative to the widespread crisis in the capitalist system, no alternative to the plundering of our states' natural resources, and no alternative in the face of neocolonialism and imperialist domination.

The Popular Alliance

Only a national and popular alliance formed of oppressed popular classes, social movements, and progressive intellectuals can meet the challenges listed above. This alliance must emerge from citizens' daily struggles and political fights to change power relations that, for the moment, are favourable to market forces. It goes without saying that this alliance is yet to be established, and its deployment cannot be envisaged in the short term. The quest for hegemony by the dominated workers and peoples—in other words the conquest of power by the demos—requires sustained ideological struggle against neoliberalism and a theoretical effort to rethink the quest for the emancipation of society and the concept of democracy.

An interest in the Sahara seems to have been a constant feature for centuries with the trans-Saharan trade (Hamani 2007). Historically all Muslim powers that have emerged on the scene have tried to control the Saharan routes as sources of considerable trade revenues. An interest in the trans-Saharan trade may explain the formation of the Sultanate of Ayar (Agadez) by recently immigrated Tuareg tribes. The conquests of Idrissa Alaoma (the sovereign of Bornou), which reached as far as Bilma in the sixteenth century, as well as those of Askia Mohamed, who reached Agadez twice (in 1500 and 1515), follow the same logic. This shows the extent to which the Sahara was a major geopolitical issue for all states in the region. This interest was rekindled well before the Conference of Berlin with the idea of the construction of a trans-Saharan railway by France in 1879 to facilitate the conquest of Central and Western Sudan.

Today Western powers show similar interest with France and the United States, who mean to control the resources of the region to the detriment of the interests of the states and their peoples, in the forefront. The future of the Sahel as well as that of West Africa is at stake. Beyond that the question of future relations with Europe also hangs in the balance. Entangled in neo-colonial relations, Europe has been unable to build real development-cooperation policies with the countries in the region. It has often contributed to maintaining dictatorial regimes and sham democracies with very little legitimacy, as evidenced by the rapid overthrow of Malian president Amadou Toumani Touré. Isn't it time to put an end to these asymmetrical relations with Europe? Isn't this an unavoidable prerequisite for any autonomous political construction? Don't the emerging countries (Brazil, Russia, India, China, and South Africa) offer an opportunity to start real construction in the Sahelo-Saharan region and on the continent as a whole? Is this not a credible alternative?

References

Abdou, I. 2008 "Nouveaux rapports de forces internationaux." Paper presented at the conference Transition Vers le Socialisme: Aspects Politique, Économique, Social et Culturel, Caracas, Venezuela, October.

Alternative Sud. 2011. *La Chine en Afrique : menace ou opportunité pour le développement? Points de vue du Sud.* Brussels: Éditions Syllepse.

Amin, S. 2012. *L'implosion du capitalisme contemporain.* Paris: Éditions Delga.

Bourgeot, A. 1995. *Les sociétés touarègues: nomadisme, identité, résistance.* Paris: Karthala.

Bourgeot, A. 1990. "Le désert quadrillé : des Touaregs au Niger." *Politique Africaine* 38, June.

Bowie, N. 2012. "L'Africom des États-Unis et la militarisation du continent africain: le combat contre l'implantation économique chinoise." Accessed April, 2012. http://www.le grandsoir.info/.

Chegrouche, L. 2010. "Géopolitique transsaharienne de l'énergie, Le jeu et l'enjeu?" *Revue de l'Énergie* 61:593.

Claudot-Hawad H. 1992. "Bandits, rebelles et partisans: vision plurielle des évènements touaregs, 1990-1992." *Politique Africaine* 46.

Dayak, M. 1992. *Touareg. La tragédie,* Paris, J.-C. Lattès.

Dembélé, D.M. 2011. *Samir Amin. Intellectuel organique au service de l'émancipation du Sud.* Dakar: CODESRIA.

Diallo, M. 2011. "Défis sécuritaires et hybridation des menaces dans la zone sahélo-saharienne." Accessed April 2013. http://www.ieps-cipsao.org.

Granvaud, R. 2012. *Areva en Afrique : Une face cachée du nucléaire Français.* Agone.

Hamani, D. 2007. "Les enjeux stratégiques autour du Sahara à travers l'histoire." Paper presented at the workshop Conflit au Nord Niger: Analyse des Enjeux Stratégiques et Impacts sur le Cadre Démocratique, Niamey, Niger 2007.

Houtart, F. 2003. "Société civile, mouvements sociaux et développement" in B.F. Tchuigoua, S. D. Sy, and A. A. Dieng, eds. *Pensée sociale critique pour le XXIe siècle. Mélanges en l'honneur de Samir Amin.*Dakar, Forum du Tiers-Monde/L'Harmattan.

Lacoste, Y. 2011. "Sahara, Perspectives et illusions géopolitiques." *Hérodote* 142.

Malti, H. 2008. "Les guerres de Bush pour le pétrole." *Algeria Watch* March 21.

Ndiaye, I. 2012. "Géopolitique du Sahara, crise généralisée du capitalisme mondialisé, crises identitaires et avenir de l'État-nation: le cas du Mali." Accessed April 2013. http://www.gabrielperi.fr.

Bagayoko-Penone, Niagalé. 2004. *Afrique: les stratégies française et américaine.* Paris: L'Harmattan.

Nkundabagenzi, F. 2005. "L'union européenne et l'Afrique. Entre contraintes et promesses." Accessed April 2013. http://www.diploweb.com/L-Union-europeenne-et-l-Afrique.html.

Obeng, K.W. 2010. "La lutte pour avoir la main mise sur le pétrole ghanéen." Accessed April 2013. http://www.twnafrica.org.

Plagnol, H. and Loncle, F. 2012. "Situation sécuritaire dans les pays de la zone sahélienne." *Rapport d'information* 4431.

Saidou, A.K. 2009. "La Problématique de la gestion post-conflit au Niger: analyse de la politique de réinsertion des ex combattants touaregs." Master's thesis, University of Ouagadougou II.

Salifou, A. 1993. *La question touarègue au Niger*. Paris: Karthala.

Taje, M. 2010. "Vulnérabilités et facteurs d'insécurité au sahel." Accessed April 2013. http://www.oecd.org/fr/csao/publications/enjeuxouest-africains.htm.

Tchokonte, S.T. 2008. "Enjeux et jeux pétroliers en Afrique : étude de l'offensive pétrolière chinoise dans le Golfe de Guinée." Master's thesis, University of Yaounde II.

Tisseron, A. 2011. "Enchevêtrements géopolitiques autour de la lutte contre le terrorisme." *Hérodote* 142.

UNDP. 2011. *Human Development Report. Sustainability and Equity: A Better Future for All*. New York: UNDP.

Zarka, P. 2012. "Pour une démocratie du movement." Accessed April 2013. http://www.gabrielperi.fr.

AFP/Jeune Afrique. 2010. "Areva Prête à ouvrir à la Chine l'exploitation de la mine d'Imouraren." November 5. *Jeune Afrique*. http://www.jeuneafrique.com.

Fratmat.info (Abidjan) 2012. "Afrique de l'Ouest: Ports de Dakar et de Conakry—La CEDEAO fait bloquer du matériel militaire malien." July 16. http://fr.allafrica.com.

Géopolitique du Sahara. Revue Hérodote 142, Troisième trimestre, 2011, http://www.herodote.org/spip.php?rubrique57.

Lettre du continent (2012), « Niger, Malaise diplomatique avec Alger », n°639, July 12 2012.

Lettre du Continent (2008) n° 551 October 30 2008.

Chapter 3

Beyond Neoliberalism: Reflections on the Democratic Development Trajectory

Kojo Opoku Aidoo

Perhaps the issue one can talk about most in contemporary Africa is development simply because, despite some six decades of efforts, most parts of the continent are still not developing. The majority of the African people, even if not technically slaves, are still denied elementary freedoms and remain imprisoned in one way or another by economic poverty, social deprivation, political tyranny, or cultural authoritarianism.

Armatya Sen (1999) explains in his *Development as Freedom* how, in a world of unprecedented increase in overall lavishness, millions of people living in the global South are still unfree. Sen has persuasively argued, and many within the development community today agree, that the main purpose of development is to spread freedom to unfree citizens. So freedom, as Sen maintains, is at once the ultimate goal of social and economic arrangements and the most efficient means of realising general welfare. Now, if development is not any mysterious undertaking, and its objectives are that clear, why is most of Africa not developing? What is wrong with the prevailing development frameworks? How might change come about? What alternatives do we have? How would the alternative development paradigms gain legitimacy and embeddedness?

Why has the economic growth performance of Sub-Saharan Africa been generally disappointing over the past fifty years? What are the lessons of success in Africa and elsewhere? Could some of the policies that proved so successful in East Asia help reverse the process of deindustrialisation that have occurred in the past three decades? Could they be the basis of its future structural transformation? These are important questions addressed by Akbar, et al. (2012). Most interestingly they conclude that though success is not assured, there is good reason to believe that policies based on lessons of successes, notably in East Asia, can be adapted successfully in African contexts. This conclusion is contentious, and I will address this a little later.

Howard (1978) approaches the problem from a dependency perspective. He notes that contemporary Africa's colonial heritage is, in brief, its dependent political economy, the underdevelopment of its productive forces, its truncated class structure, and finally its pessimistic prognosis for progressive political policies in such a context. The problem for Howard remains how Africa will overcome its colonial heritage and reorient it on the trajectory to integrated economic, social, and political development. Indeed, though the petty bourgeoisie is the politically dominant class in Africa, it has no real role in the productive process. This explains why, according to Howard, Africa is experiencing an uncertain historical movement whose direction and meaning will be defined and redefined through practice.

Two quotations from Walter Rodney and Claude Ake are in order here—two Africanist scholars whose immense theoretical contribution to Africa's struggles to develop have been vindicated by the current trend of global economy and Africa's marginalisation. It is important to note that Rodney published his path-breaking *How Europe Underdeveloped Africa* some forty years ago, in 1972. In the preface he wrote, "African development is possible only on the basis of a radical break with the international capitalist system, which has been the principal agency of underdevelopment of Africa over the last five centuries" (Rodney 2012). In *Democracy and Development in Africa*, Claude Ake wrote:

Development will have to take the people as they are, not as they ought to be in someone else's image of the world. The only way forward for Africans is for them to move forward on their own steam in accordance with their values. This is the way to make the African the agents, means and end of development. (Ake 2001)

These two quotations summarise the central theoretical and ideological message of this chapter: there must be a decisive and radical break with international capitalism and endogenous development in tandem! That, in a nutshell, would be the credible trajectory to sustainable development in Africa.

Now, to set the tone and the background, a few preliminary observations are in order about the development frameworks that have been in vogue in post-colonial Africa. To understand the political economy and dynamics of African development, we must begin with an appreciation of the material base: African economies until recently remained highly statist—that is, state dominated. African economies and their productive forces are underdeveloped, and their economic surplus is meagre; they are highly dependent on the former colonial powers, and their economies are highly disarticulated. Over half a century of preoccupation with development has yielded largely stagnation, regression, or worse. And the tragic consequences of this are all around us: a rising wave of poverty; decaying public utilities and collapsing infrastructure; social tensions and political turmoil; and, until recently, premonitions of inevitable drift into conflict and violence.

This leads me to my second observation: because of these demoralising economic conditions, I often hear some people defend the idea that Africa, in order to develop, must follow some "stages" or meet some "conditions." I disagree because that approach seeks to get the African people to develop against themselves. It tends to appropriate the people's right to develop themselves, which is a form of social violence and alienation. Contrary to modernisation theory and its variants, I think we need to follow the processes and dynamics of African development to see where it might lead. That does not imply passivity; rather it means constantly analysing the configuration of social forces in Africa—the contradictions, their potentialities, agendas, struggles, and the possible outcomes.

The third observation is that the prevailing development paradigms in contemporary Africa appear so well established, so apparently plausible, and so embedded and legitimised in the existing structuring of power that the very idea of a possible alternative system of development seems frivolous or even utopian. That legitimisation and embeddedness constitute the most important obstacle to the emergence of alternative paradigms in Africa. It is therefore important to deal with the confusions, irrelevances, ambiguities, contradictions, antinomies, frills, and distortions that stand in the way of alternative systems of development.

Fourth, development is not economic growth as development economists like Rostow (1960) and Arthur Lewis (1954), in defending the so-called "expanding capitalist nucleus perspective," wanted us to believe even though economic growth does to some degree determine its possibility. But as we have seen in all too many cases in postcolonial Africa and indeed globally, there can be growth without development.

Fifth, development is not a project but a process, one in which "people create and recreate themselves and their life circumstances to realise higher levels of civilisation in accordance with their own choices and values" (Nnaemeka, 2009). So development is something people must do for themselves—i.e., people must be the agents, means, and end of development. In other words development is a lived experience and not a received experience. So it is not possible to have development by proxy. Africans must develop themselves or not at all.

Sixth, development paradigms should best be seen as discourses, or theories that serve to reinforce dominant global political interests. In contrast to definitions that conceive of development as an objective phenomenon that occurs when national economies grow (Lewis 1954), societies modernise (Rostow 1960), or social, economic, and political freedoms expand (Sen 1999), a discursive definition of development argues that the essence of development is the exercise of power by rich nations over poor nations. Development discourses become institutionalised in international development agencies. These agencies then encourage Southern nations to follow supposedly value-neutral paths to prosperity such as agricultural modernisation and market liberalisation. Regardless of whether or not these policies can deliver their promised benefits, they do reflect the political and economic interests of the global North. Given these assumptions, development policymaking and research have tended to focus more on policy options (technical, market, institutional) and less on domestic political issues and policy processes. Yet despite decades of efforts, Africa remains languid and underdeveloped. This calls therefore for discourse deconstruction. In some way discursive definitions of development expose the architecture of power that underlies development policy (Escobar 1995). And in the last few years, a domestic-politics school has emerged to correct the lopsidedness in the prevailing development thinking.

A final observation: Development strategies and policies do not simply emerge and get implemented, their feasibility and success determined by their formal character. On the contrary development strategies and policies are made by a government in office and a political elite in power in a historical state, and with a particular configuration of social forces. Thus we cannot comprehend development strategies and policies, let alone their potential, without referring constantly to the character of the state, the dynamics of the social forces in which it is embedded, and the kind of politics it engenders. The meaning of all this is that development is politically charged and politically driven.

Development Politics and History in Postcolonial Africa

There have been two types of development initiatives in postindependence Africa, namely initiatives by Africa and initiatives for Africa (Baah 2003). The former refers to endogenous efforts or initiatives that were designed and implemented *by* African countries after independence. The second relates to initiatives that are designed *for* Africa and implemented through international financial institutions. The two initiatives have different characteristics.

Africa-owned initiatives were people-centred. They succeeded, to some extent, in terms of human development. Unfortunately the period during which Africans had the opportunity to initiate their own development policies was very short, lasting less than a decade from independence (between 1960 and 1970). Since then "all initiatives have been designed by 'aliens' for Africa and they have all failed" (Baah 2003). The failure is evidenced by the ever-growing debt and increased incidence of poverty, unfreedom, and disempowerment on the African continent even if sub-Saharan Africa has shown strong levels of economic growth over the last ten years.

It must be pointed out that the development paradigms in fashion tend to be ahistorical and atheoretical in that they tend to stress domestic constraints to the neglect of the externalities that contrived to produce underdevelopment and the dependency often highlighted in the writings and language of the dependency school. They tend to ignore the fact that Africa's present is shaped by her colonial experience and that the integration of Africa's colonial economies into the world's capitalist system in the late nineteenth and early twentieth centuries had two contradictory effects. The integration of Africa into the global capitalist system resulted in its development as a peripheral capitalist economy, but concomitant with that development is the underdevelopment of her capitalist potential. Thus colonial exploitation prevented Africa from developing full capitalism. The ramifications of this historical legacy are deep, and it is important to recognise them in order to grasp fully the processes, travails, and dynamics of contemporary African (under)development.

There is, however, another reason why Africa has not developed full capitalism. It has to do with the continent's trade mentality. A quick historical detour will further clarify this point. The industrial revolution in England around 1733 rapidly transformed the English political economy but also posed challenges to the rest of the world. Contrary to the official rhetoric of free traders and the official history of capitalism, England and the USA both developed under protectionism. Bairoch has observed that the USA is "the mother country and bastion of modern protectionism" and that "those who don't obey the rules win" (Bairoch 1993; see also Chang 2002). Regarding the industrial revolution in England, Inikori (2002) has shown with a luxury of details that the Atlantic trade has financed it and in some ways is responsible for the industrialisation of England.

Be that as it may, faced with the challenge posed by the emergence of capitalist industrialism, some nations tried to imitate the English experience while others made many efforts to open to international trade in a free trade framework. Interestingly those nations that imitated became successful while those that simply resorted to free trade failed to achieve a measure of economic growth (here reference is being made to the distinction between countries that imitated the industrial revolution and those that, in line with the theory of comparative advantage, simply traded while still remaining pre-industrial).

The first lesson of development history, therefore, is that nations that try to imitate do better than those with trade mentality, which is what Africa has! And this alone gave a big lie to the theory of comparative advantage. Instead of being left to its own devices and to imitate the process of industrialisation, Africa has been confined to agrarianism with no forward and backward linkages. One important ramification of the lack of develeepent of full capitalism has been that the emergence of a state in most Africa that is an montrosity that undermines development.

A fully developed capitalist society has an inbuilt tendency to legitimise capitalist exchange and production through commodity fetishism. Market society has its own logic that determines its own form of government and administration and its political ideology. This is reflected in the fit of the capitalist economy and liberal government in Adam Smith's work (Smith 1776). The affinity between the core values of the market and liberal democracy can be seen clearly by reflecting on the presuppositions of commodity production and exchange. The commodity bearers act self-interestedly and are formally free and equal. In fact in the market, commodity bearers appear free and equal, and labour power seems fully paid for; the actions of commodity bearers constitute what looks like a system of natural laws. These core values of formal freedom and equality, egotism, and rule of private property are reproduced on the political sphere in bourgeois politics: political competitors are formally free and equal and may compete for office in conditions that are formally the same. This formal equal access gives the impression of objectivity, so the government arising from competition seems legitimate. The state in a capitalist society then becomes an autonomous public force that operates in conformity with the rule of law. The rule of law epitomises the political form under capitalism as the summation of the conditions of market society and of the realisation of the law of value.

The African condition is entirely different, and that explains why the emerging political systems on the continent lack the essential elements of liberalism. The state that emerged in independent Africa in most cases is not an objective public force rising above particular interests and groups to express the corporate identity of political society. It lacks autonomy. The typical African state tends to claim near-absolute power; it is tendentially authoritarian and, in the absence of substantive checks and balances, virtually arbitrary. Consequently, for the most part, the postcolonial state and its politics have been so dysfunctional, it has not allowed development projects to take off. As Ake (2001) has noted, the ideology of development in the postcolonial period has been exploited as a means of reproducing political hegemony; it got limited attention and served hardly any purpose as a framework for economic transformation.

Of course development plans were written and proclaimed. But what passed for development plans were aggregations of projects and objectives informed by the latest fads of the international development community such as import substitution and export promotion. As these fads changed in the larger world, so they were abandoned in Africa. Ake (2001) has argued, and I share his view, the main obstacle to development in Africa is political; the point is not so much that the development project has failed as that it never got started in the first place. Ake elaborates on that point with reference to the conflict over development agendas between Africa's leaders and the international development agencies. This conflict has stalled the development project by leaving African leaders trapped in the dilemma of choosing between an endogenous agenda they cannot find the means to implement and an exogenous agenda they cannot bring themselves to accept, between what they want to do and what they must do. The late Claude Ake (1996) has interrogated these confusions of agendas, improbable strategies as well as the blocked options and the residual options.

The Confusion of Agendas

Despite five decades of preoccupation with development, the economies of most African nations are still stagnating or regressing. For most Africans incomes are lower than they were some decades ago, health prospects are poorer, malnourishment is widespread, and infrastructures and social institutions are breaking down. For example, about 65 percent of Africans are said to be living below the poverty line of two dollars a day, and Africa's share of global trade is no more than 3.5 percent, which renders African economies almost irrelevant to world trade. An array of factors have been offered to explain the apparent failure of development in Africa including the colonial legacy, sociological pluralism (namely the multiplicity of ethnicities), corruption, poor planning and incompetent management, limited inflow of foreign capital, and low levels of saving and investment.

Alone or in combination, these factors are serious impediments to development, but Ake (2001) contends the problem is not that development has failed, but it was never really on the agenda. He maintains that political conditions in Africa are the greatest impediment to development. Ake traces the evolution and failure of development policies including the IMF stabilisation programmes that have dominated international efforts. He identifies the root causes of the problem in the authoritarian political structure of the African states derived from the previous colonial entities. Ake sketches the alternatives that are struggling to emerge from calamitous failure—for example, economic development based on traditional agriculture, political development based on the decentralisation of power, and reliance on indigenous communities that have been providing some measure of refuge from the coercive power of the central state. By 1985, however, Africa was no longer experiencing any ordinary development challenges; she was rather in a crisis, and her very survival was in question. Strategies from below were not formulated, nor was there commitment from above to development. Since then sub-Saharan Africa has been experiencing the deepest and most protracted crises in modern history. These crises have been phenomenally very harsh, tragic, and debilitating.

> In 1986, an important seminar took place in Uppsala, Sweden. Its purpose was to provide a platform for a cross section of African scholars and leaders, which included A.M. Babu, Joseph Ki-Zerbo, Changa Macho, Wamba dia Wamba and Goran Hyden. They were to discuss alternative development strategies for Africa's future. (Bennaars 1993, 101)

The participants at this seminar tried to seek African solutions to African problems. That was commendable because I also think that until Africans are left to their own devices and African solutions are found to African problems, there will be no deliverance for the African states.

Five years later "the ideas discussed at the Uppsala seminar found a more vigorous expression…in the *African Charter for Popular Participation and Transformation* (Arusha 1990). Underlying the charter was a vision of a new Africa. This vision seeks to advocate human development and economic justice, democracy and accountability, and above all popular participation. At the same time, it vows to fight despotism, authoritarianism, and kleptocracy" (Nnaemeka 2009).

To date there have been four landmark strategies that together give some indication as to how Africa's preferred development agenda emerged in the 1980s and the early 1990s. These are:

- The Lagos Plan of Action for the Economic Development of Africa 1980-2000 and the Final Act of Lagos (1980).
- Africa's Priority Programme for Economic Recovery 1986-1990 (APPER), which was later converted into the United Nations Programme of Action for Africa's Economic Recovery and Development (UN-PAAERD) (1986).
- The African Alternative Framework to Structural Adjustment Programme for Socio-Economic Recovery and Transformation (AAF-SAP) (1989).
- The African Charter for Popular Participation for Development (1990) versus The United Nations New Agenda for the Development of Africa in the 1990s (UN-NADAF) (1991).

It is important to recognise that Africa has experimented with almost every conceivable development paradigm. "For example, African socialism was practiced in Tanzania and certain parts of Africa; Marxist-Leninist Socialism was practiced in Mozambique under Machel, in Ethiopia under Mengistu and experimented in Angola; modernization theories including the expanding capitalist nucleus perspective that Arthur Lewis posted to Ghana and which the UNDP tried to implement; the basic needs approach, paradigms based on dependency theory and various neoliberal approaches were practiced as well.

Nonetheless, despite five decades of preoccupation with development in Africa, the economies of most African nations are still stagnating or regressing. My argument is that political conditions in Africa are the greatest impediment to development. I have identified the root causes of the problem in the authoritarian political structure of the African states derived from the previous colonial entities. I think Africa cannot escape from underdevelopment until public policy becomes an expression of people's democratic will and connects with their social needs. What is required is an entirely new paradigm with a new strategy or model that connects with the people's democratic aspirations and social needs— a paradigm whose strategy makes the African people the agents, the means, and the end of the development. Before dealing with this new strategy, I will say a word about the neoliberal paradigm and why it is an improbable strategy or a blocked option.

The Improbable Strategy or a Blocked Option

Africa's development via neoliberal approaches appears effectively blocked. The promised benefits of neoliberalism have failed to materialise at least for the majority of African people. The experiences of the decades between the two world wars have taught us that the economic and political fate of Africa could not safely be delegated to unregulated, free-market systems since that trajectory leads to economic instability, intermittent depression, and political chaos.

In the aftermath of World War II, national economies, even those in which markets played very powerful roles, were placed under the ultimate control of governments, and international economic relations were deliberately managed by the International Monetary Fund and World Bank. Significant strides were made then in economic recovery and prosperity. And, as Crotty (2000) argues, in discussing the structural contradictions of contemporary capitalism, the global prosperity that characterised the quarter century following the Second World War reinforced belief in the wisdom of the social regulation of economic affairs.

The attempts at dealing with the structural defects in African economies in the late 1970s have led to the rolling back of the economic regulatory power of the state, replacing conscious societal control with the invisible hand of unregulated markets. Apologists of neoliberalism anticipated that this new laissez-faire epoch would radically improve economic performance in African countries. Regrettably, more than two decades after the neoliberal efforts, the promised benefits have yet to materialise, at least for the majority of the

African masses. According to Crotty (2000), during this period of pervasive liberalism global income growth has plummeted, as has the rate of capital accumulation; productivity growth has deteriorated, real wage growth has declined, average unemployment has risen, inequality has increased in most countries, real interest rates are higher; financial crises erupt with increasing regularity; and less-developed nations outside East Asia have fallen even further behind the advanced nations.

So the paths of deregulation, liberalisation, privatisation, and global economic integration to development have been blocked, and it looks almost impossible for Africa to achieve a measure of development via that route. What liberalism and globalisation have succeeded in doing is ensconcing Africa in her role as exporter of primary products within the global political economy, thus consolidating her underdeveloped and dependent status. What Africa requires is radical economic and political transformation.

But the problem is bigger than is posed: Africa's incorporation into the global capitalist system and its assignment to produce raw materials to feed industries in the industrial North has meant her emergence as a monocrop agrarian continent and therefore the underdevelopment of her capitalist potential. However, the development of Africa's capitalist potential is effectively blocked not just by monocropism and agrarianisation but also through processes of marginalisation by the development of science, technology, and production that are delinking the industrial economies from primary economies. By and large, primary products are being displaced by synthetic materials that are often stronger, more versatile, and easier to work with. Simultaneously the raw-material content of goods has been decreasing in a continuous process of dematerialisation. The industrial nations are no longer as dependent on primary products as they used to be. The general implication has been that primary producers are undermined, commodity prices are depressed, export earnings are diminishing, and African states are been driven deeper into debt.

These developments objectify the North-South divide and the marginalisation of Africa; above all they block Africa's potential to develop within the world capitalist system. I will not go into Hernando de Soto's arguments about why some countries succeed at capitalism while others fail. De Soto (2000) finds it actually has everything to do with the legal structure of property. Every developed nation in the world at one time went through the transformation from predominantly informal, extralegal ownership to a formal, unified legal property system. In de Soto's scheme of things, in Africa we have not created the system that allows people to leverage property into wealth.

Let me reiterate nonetheless that the integration of Africa's colonial economies into the world's capitalist system in the late nineteenth and early twentieth centuries had two contradictory effects: integration into the global capitalist system resulted in its development as a peripheral capitalist economy, but concomitant with that development it also resulted in the underdevelopment of Africa's capitalist potential. During the colonial period, African countries underwent a transition from their various precapitalist social formations to quasi-capitalist organisations of production. Such a transition to capitalism was incomplete, and that incompleteness was a result of the very structures of the world capitalist system that prevented the formation of a developed capitalist mode of production in the peripheral areas.

It is important also to stress here that peripheral capitalist societies are underdeveloped because the forces for change unleashed by their contacts with core capitalist countries—especially the development of new social groupings with the potential to become indigenous, productive capitalists—are constrained by their externally oriented economies. This new social force cannot imitate the model of capitalist development in the Western world. The structure of the global capitalist system, reinforced by production organised primarily for export, restricts them. The situation is worst if the peripheral countries underwent colonial rule as well because then they are also constrained by a foreign state structure that regulates their internal economic development in its own interests or at least, as Howard argues, in the interests of its own bourgeoisie.

To conclude this aspect, let me say that a peripheral economy that has been under colonial dependency is characterised by a high degree of integration into the world capitalist system but a low degree of development of the capitalist mode of production internally. So what are the residual options, if any?

The Residual-Options Agenda for the future

The capitalist pathway, as I have said, is blocked, and any further movement along that path will only consolidate the peripheral underdeveloped and dependent status of Africa. So what is to be done? In the past Africa has tended to proceed ad hoc, reacting to apparent opportunities but by and large driven by pressures in the domestic and global environments in what has proved to be a journey without maps to an uncertain destination. A vision is clearly required, but it has to evolve without repeating the old ways of proceeding. Clear, compelling, and viable socioeconomic and political alternatives are needed. What Africa needs at this time in history is a development strategy that proceeds in daily response to the practical needs of the people. It must be endogenous and self-reliant; it must not be driven by foreign loans and foreign technology, foreign investment, or foreign trade. It must rely on an assured and gradually expanding domestic market; it should obliterate the dichotomy between industry and agriculture, urban and rural, and prioritise internal balance and autocentrism. This is what I call *democratic development*.

A development strategy of this type will require radically different ways of implementation from what is currently the practice. It will require a large number of new institutions at the grassroots level—institutions for human development and empowerment so ordinary people can manage their own development. Democratic development will place a great deal of emphasis on human development, to enhance the capacity of people to develop themselves, including illiteracy eradication, higher levels of education, health enhancement, skill development, management training, etc. The successful East Asian nations, such as South Korea, used this human-development approach to good effect. All of them invested heavily in education, for example.

Furthermore, if Africa adopts the principle of democratic development then development will have to be construed initially as rural development and, more specifically, as agricultural development. Approximately 70 percent of African peoples are rural dwellers and make their livelihoods predominantly from agricultural activities (Ake 2000). Once the concept of development is assimilated into the concept of rural development, the traditional dichotomy between agriculture and industrialisation might disappear.

Indeed under democratic development, a policy of rural industrialisation will be integrated with agricultural development as part of a general strategy of rural development. And this can be pursued mainly in self-reliance, driven by farmers' incomes and the multiplier effect of the linkages between farm and nonfarm incomes. There will be expansion in the forward, backward, and consumer-demand linkages. This will engender greater integration of rural and urban development that will pay special attention to the informal sector, which is quite huge in African countries. In a nutshell the strategy of democratic development will clearly privilege an economy in which the majority of the African people are engaged.

The principle of democratic development posits that ordinary people must possess their own development, which implies they have to be its agents as well as its means and ends. To own their development, African people have to accept self-reliance; they have to be willing to bear the burden of their own development even when they are technically limited and poor for there is no other way of owning one's development. Only by doing so can Africans can break from the prevailing patterns of development that tendentially pervert development into an exercise in alienation.

The development alternative I have in mind is what some political economists call *development from below*. That means development not from above, or by the state, but from ordinary citizens through their own self-advancement. It calls for a change in surplus accumulation strategy. And that involves what I call the *promotion of mass prosperity*, or the democratisation of wealth creation and accumulation. China has followed this strategy since 1979. It involves using the prosperous masses as Africa's entering wedge into industrialism. It basically extends the fostering of development from below this time in industry, which is the ultimate goal in allowing peasant accumulation of surpluses in the first place. And the Chinese example shows it works wonders.

I am convinced that elite-led development will never work in contemporary Africa. Globally and historically the social consequence has always been the needless impoverishment of millions of peasants to enrich a few political and financial elites. This strategy involving allowing the peasant and primary producers to prosper from their efforts, to accumulate wealth, is what I call, for want of a better term, the *freedom to prosper policy*. Once this decision has been made, a massive redistribution of income favouring the productive sections of society, the peasantry for example, is the expected outcome. All state agencies will have to do is to guide the new wealth into industrial areas strategic to the production of more national wealth as the Chinese have been doing for more than three decades. The states in Africa as presently constituted will never develop the continent. Only the people will. The state needs to create conditions for prosperity and wealth creation, guide this wealth into industrialism, and then get the hell out of the way. The African people will do the rest.

As pointed out earlier, it is misleading to say development has failed in Africa. To be sure, development has failed in Africa but only because it has never started in the first place due to disempowering political conditions. It can start, and it can succeed. What is required is an entirely new paradigm with a new strategy or model that connects with the people's democratic aspirations and social needs—in other words democratic development, a paradigm whose strategy makes the African people the agents, means, and ends of the development taking place in their domain. The African people must develop themselves or not at all.

References

Akbar N., K. Botchwey, H. Stein, and J.E. Stiglitz. 2012. *Good Growth and Governance in Africa. Rethinking Development Strategies*. Oxford, Oxford University Press.

Ake, C. 2000. *The Feasibility of Democracy in Africa*. Dakar: Codesria.

Ake, C. 2001. *Democracy and Development in Africa*. Ibadan: Spectrum Books.

Baah, A. 2003. "History of African Development Initiatives." Paper presented at Africa Labour Research Network Workshop, Johannesburg, May 22-23, 2003.

Bairoch, P. 1995. *Economics and World History: Myths and Paradoxes*. Chicago: University of Chicago Press.

Bennaars, G.A. 1993. *Ethics, Education and Development. An Introductory Text for Students in Colleges and Universities*. Nairobi: East African Educational Publishers, Ltd.

Chang, H.-J. 2002. *Kicking Away the Ladder. Development Strategy in Historical Perspective*. London: Anthem Press.

Crotty, J. 2000. "Structural Contradictions of Current Capitalism. A Keynes-Marx-Schumpeter Analysis." Paper presented at the Globalization, Structural Change and Income Distribution conference, Chennai, India, December 2000.

De Soto, H. 2000. *The Mystery of Capital: Why Capitalism Triumphs in the West and Fails Everywhere Else*. New York, Basic Books.

Escobar, A. 1995. *Encountering Development: The Making and Unmaking of the Third World*. Princeton: Princeton University Press.

Howard, R.E. 1978. *Colonialism and Underdevelopment in Ghana*. London: Croom Helm.

Hyden, G. 1980. *Beyond Ujaama in Tanzania underdevelopment and an uncaptured peasantry.* Berkeley and Los Angeles: University of California Press.

Inikori, J. 2002. *Africans and the Industrial Revolution in England. A Study in International. Trade and Economic Development.* Cambridge, Cambridge University Press.

Lewis, A. W. "Economic Development with Unlimited Supplies of Labor." *Manchester School of Economic and Social Studies* 22, 2 (1954): 139–91.

Lewis, A.W. 1969. *Some aspects of economic development.* Accra, Ghana Pub. Corp.

Nnaemeka, A.N. "Towards an Alternative Development Paradigm for Africa." *Journal of Social Sciences* 21, 1 (2009): 39-48.

Rostow W.W. 1960. *The Stage of Economic Growth: A Non-Communist Manifesto.* Cambridge: Cambridge University Press.

Rodney, W.A. 2012. *How Europe Underdeveloped Africa.* Oxford/Dakar, Pambazuka Press and CODESRIA.

Smith, A. 1776. *An Inquiry into the Nature and Causes of the* Wealth of Nations. London: W. Strahan and T. Cadell.

Sen, A. 1999. *Development as Freedom.* Cambridge, Cambridge University Press.

CHAPTER 4

RETHINKING AFRICAN DEVELOPMENT: A GENDER-RESPONSIVE GOVERNANCE AGENDA

Kehinde Olusola Olayode

The missing link in promoting gender equality in Africa is to understand effectively the linkages between gender inequalities and African development and to formulate strategies and policies that reflect these linkages. Gender equality has an intrinsic value that produces positive outcomes in development. In the search for alternatives to African development, the challenge consists of promoting development based on gender equality and on full participation of both men and women whatever their social characteristics or origins. There can be no relevant alternatives for Africa without the promotion of gender equality. If positive outcomes are to be achieved in development, African women, who constitute more than half of the population, must be counted as full development partners. There is therefore an urgent need to target development policies because gender is a development issue and a development goal in its own right.

The African continent is well endowed with abundant resources—natural, cultural, and human. However, its peoples remain poor, and poverty affects African women most severely. Part of what makes them poor are social inequalities and the lack of opportunities they face solely because of their gender. Empirical data show 60 percent of Africans live below the poverty level, many of who live on less than two US dollars per day. Unemployment and underemployment affect a large share of the labour force (Aina 2008). Women are worse hit mainly because they lack access to critical resources—education, capital, entrepreneurial skills, and, most importantly, a lack of control over the use of their valuable time. Hence the percentage of women remains predominantly high among the core poor. Poverty wears a woman's face.

Although gender inequality exists in most societies around the world to differing extents, the combined devastating effects of poverty, discrimination, and lack of opportunity affect African women in multiple ways from their economic standing (income levels, rights to own property, access to finance) to their social well-being (access to health services and education) and their prospects for better living conditions (heavy household-work burdens, ability to secure employment or be self-employed).

Another negative consequence of the constraints is women's low participation in national and regional policy making. Their invisibility in national statistics and their low participation in development planning means issues of concern to women are neglected in the design and implementation of many development policies and programmes.

Gender discrimination in access to and control over resources such as land, agricultural inputs, extension services, and employment persist in many African countries where women get land-property rights through their husbands as long as the marriages endure. They generally lose those rights when they are divorced or widowed. As women are the backbone of agriculture, gender inequalities in access to land and agricultural inputs reduce agricultural productivity. Agriculture is a very important sector of African economy, employing about 60 percent of the population and contributing a significant percentage of the GDP. Low agricultural productivity reduces growth and food security, increasing the vulnerability and poverty of the population (UNDP 2008). Because of their low educational levels, women and girls are found mainly in low-skills and low-paying jobs.

The World Bank has identified gender equality and women empowerment (GEWE) as one of the key constituent elements of primary development goals and poverty reduction. The promotion of women's empowerment as a development goal is based on a dual argument: that social justice is an important aspect of human welfare and is intrinsically worth pursuing and that women's empowerment is a means to other ends. A policy research report by the World Bank (2000), for example, identifies gender equality as both a development objective in itself and a means to promoting growth, reducing poverty, and promoting better governance. A similar dual rationale for supporting women's empowerment has been articulated in the policy statements put forth at several high-level international conferences in the past decade (e.g., the Beijing Platform for Action, the Beijing+5 declaration and resolution, the Cairo Programme of Action, the Millennium Declaration, and the Convention on the Elimination of All Forms of Discrimination against Women [CEDAW]).

As the gender variable enters the development equation, attention is drawn to a better understanding of gender relations, particularly the unequal power distribution between women and men across societies. Gender equality does not ignore the biological differences between men and women (especially their reproductive roles); rather it helps us appreciate the uniqueness of each gender group and the importance of bringing the different needs and priorities of both women and men into development agendas, thereby helping us focus on gender differences in social arrangements, gender equity, and social justice, which are at the heart of sustainable development. According to a UNDP report (1995), "development that is not engendered is endangered." Therefore, engendering national development is to ensure that both men and women are free to develop their full potentials and are able to make choices without restrictive gender roles. It thus follows that the needs and interests of women and men are to be equally valued and protected if any nation is to achieve sustainable development.

Incorporating gender perspectives into governance not only facilitates an improvement of women's situations and increased gender equality but contributes to positive outcomes in achieving the goal of good governance. Gender-responsive governance is crucial for achieving the goals of poverty reduction in Africa. The significant differences in voice, opportunity, and outcome between different groups in society, including between women and men, is a critical factor to address in poverty-reduction strategies. It is a matter of concern that much of the focus on governance continues to be solely in terms of political aspects, overlooking the importance of social and economic empowerment and equality between women and men for sustainable development (Ashworth 1994).

This chapter addresses the nexus between gender-responsive governance and development issues in Africa. It attempts to answer the following questions: Is governance gender neutral? Are women's different needs and priorities taken into account when governance decisions and actions are taken? What are the various components of gender-responsive governance? How could gender dimension be mainstreamed into governance and developmental issues?

Conceptual Clarifications

Gender and Sex

Gender refers to both women and men and the relations between them. Promotion of gender equality should therefore concern and engage men as well as women. *Gender* refers to socially constructed roles and socially learned behaviours and expectations associated with masculinity and femininity. Women differ from men biologically, but all cultures interpret and elaborate these innate biological differences into a set of social expectations about what behaviours and activities are appropriate and what rights, resources, and power they possess (World Bank 2001). *Sex* refers to the biological characteristics that distinguish human beings as female or male (March, Smyth, and Mukhopadhyay 1999). Sex is determined at birth and is relatively fixed; it does not change over time nor across countries and across cultures. Gender roles are learned through sociali sation processes, they are not fixed but are changeable. Gender roles are not biologically determined but vary according to culture and epoch and even for individuals during the courses of their lives.

Governance

While there is no commonly acceptable definition of *governance*, the word refers essentially to the manner in which power is exercised and distributed in society, how decisions are made, and how citizens have their say. Governance is essentially the system of processes, mechanisms, and institutions through which societies organise interactions among citizens as well as between citizens and their rulers and make choices among their often-competing interests to meet their different needs. It touches upon issues such as interaction between the state and civil society, the legal framework, public administration, economic development, development policies, peace, and security. Characteristics of governance include effectiveness, transparency, accountability, predictability, integrity, equity, and participation.

Governance is presumed to be gender neutral. However, the discourse, procedures, structures, and functions of governance remain heavily skewed in favour of men in general. This unequal sharing of power leads to an unequal sharing of resources—time, incomes, and property—between men and women. The consequences of this maldistribution are evident in the disproportionately high number of women who are illiterate and living in extreme poverty. Redressing these inequalities requires a gendered analysis of the processes and structures of governance. Such an analysis suggests that the family (or household) and the community are sites of governance in that they are spaces where people interact and in which power is exercised.

Gender-Responsive Governance

Gender-responsive governance means equal participation of women and men in decision-making processes, equal representation in governance, and equal access to benefits and opportunities. Thus, when constructing policies and programs, we must keep a gender-mainstreaming perspective to ensure balanced representation, remove barriers to women's participation, and ensure the integration of gender issues and concerns in decision making, implementation, monitoring, and evaluation of all governance initiatives. A gender analysis of governance highlights the critical interdependence between participation, representation, and responsiveness. Balanced participation is an important step toward improving the quality of governance. For this to happen, we need well-conceived social inclusion and equity-oriented policies in all areas, pursued by a critical mass of social-equity-oriented women and men who should occupy key positions in judiciary, executive, and legislative functions of the state (European Commission 1992).

Gender-sensitive governance seeks to ensure that both women and men have equal access to and control over the resources and services. The integration of a gender approach into policy, planning, and management will make development not only more equitable but also more effective. Consequently allocation of resources to women may benefit a wider development scope in which the interests of women and men are served in a more balanced way. Getting women into the mainstream of public office and the bureaucracy also is a vital part of engendering governance (Sen and Grown 1988).

Gender and African Development Agenda: Defining the Problem

Promoting gender equality and women's empowerment is essential to achieving human development, poverty eradication, and sustained economic growth on the African continent. The continued existence of disparities between women and men in access to and control over resources, and the overt discrimination against women throughout history, are now seen as cogs in the wheel of national and international development agendas (González, Jurado, and Naldini 2000). The ages-long restrictions placed on women's life choices and opportunities hinder not only their growth but the development of nations. No wonder countries with wide gender gaps exhibit poor indicators of growth and well-being—poor nutrition, high maternal-mortality rates, high infant-mortality rates, high poverty rates, low life expectancies; low levels of education; and high HIV/AIDS prevalence rates. All these are symptomatic of underdevelopment (World Bank 2002). Importantly, the achievement of gender equality is bound up with all other goals of sustainable development such as good governance, poverty reduction, environmental sustainability, and human rights.

With only three years until the Millennium Development Goals' (MDGs) target date of 2015, many African states continue to face development crises including high levels of poverty, corruption, bad governance, poor health indicators, environmental degradations, eroding educational systems, economic crises, and, worst, violent conflicts. Gender conditions are central to the African-development debate, in particular the status of African women. It is now popularly agreed that the achievement of all other MDG goals is hinged on the achievement of MDG goal number three: to promote gender equality and empower women. Promoting gender equality in policy making, implementation, monitoring, and evaluation is a must if Africa is to extricate itself from poverty and underdevelopment. For this to happen, we must consider gender as a category of analysis at the theoretical, conceptual, and empirical levels of any policy making in Africa. Assessment of the implementation of MDGs three years from the deadline shows that while all regions are making progress, sub-Saharan African countries lag behind and are not likely to achieve the MDGs during the agreed-upon timeframe (Olayode 2011).

Another facet of the linkages between gender, poverty, and development in Africa is the gender inequalities in the division of labour. In African countries, like in most countries worldwide, women and girls are primarily responsible for the domestic work of caring for and maintaining the family and its members—in other words the labour force and the human capital essential to the functioning of the economy and the society. Given the lacking or poor basic social infrastructure such as water, energy, and transportation, African women spend long hours fetching water, collecting wood, and processing food. Women's workloads lead to their time and energy poverty due to their social responsibilities of performing simultaneously reproductive, productive, and community tasks. They also have to make tradeoffs between those tasks. Women's important domestic work, as well as their contributions to their households' production and the economy, is not only unpaid; it is not measured, nor is it taken into consideration in national accounts. As a result their critical needs related to the burden of unpaid work are overlooked in the policy-making and implementation processes.

Although women's participation in the market economy has increased, especially in the informal sector, at the same time women's domestic workloads have not declined. Women continue to be primarily responsible for such activities as the care of children and elderly household members, cooking and cleaning, fetching water and firewood, and managing households in general. Thus the existence of gender-related barriers can thwart the economic potential of women owing to their adverse impact on enterprise development, productivity, and competitiveness (Aina and Olayode 2011).

Widespread poverty remains the major challenge to development efforts in Africa. This is revealed by phenomena like unemployment, malnutrition, illiteracy, low status of women, environmental degradation, and limited access to social and health services including reproductive health services (see "Some Facts" in box below). The outcome of these poverty-generated conditions includes high levels of fertility, morbidity, and mortality and low economic productivity. Sustained economic growth and development are essential to poverty eradication, and, more importantly, women empowerment is now seen as an entry point to gender equality in society. A focus on gender equality is essential for adequate analysis of the causes and impacts of poverty and the identification of effective strategies to eradicate poverty. Central to such a focus is attention to gender perspectives including the equitable participation of women (Aina 2008).

Some Facts[1]

- Women own less than 1 percent of the African continent's landmass.
- Women farmers receive only 1 percent of total credit for agriculture.
- An African woman's average workday lasts 50 percent longer than that of a man.
- Only 51 percent of females over age fifteen in Africa are able to read and write compared to 67 percent of males.
- Three-quarters of all Africans between the ages of fifteen and twenty-four who are HIV-positive are women.
- A pregnant woman in Africa is 180 times more likely to die of pregnancy complications than a woman in Western Europe.
- Limited education and employment opportunities for women in Africa reduce annual per capita growth by 0.8 percent. Had this growth taken place, Africa's economies would have doubled over the past thirty years.

---

1 African Partnership Forum Support Unit 2007

Gender and Development: From WID to GAD

The initial efforts made to integrate the women's question into the development process have tended to focus exclusively on women. This was the case with the women in development (WID) approach of the 1970s (i.e., the women-empowerment paradigm). Aside from the feminist movement of the 1960s in Europe and America, the first international policy push for the WID agenda came from the United Nations' International Year of Women (1975) and the International Women's Decade (1976–85), which led to the establishment of women's ministries in many of its member countries and the adoption of WID policies by donor agencies, governments, and NGOs (Martinussen 1997).

Under WID women were perceived as neglected economic resources who had been ignored or sidelined into the nonproductive sector as caregivers and housewives. WID advocates argued that if women were incorporated into development processes, they would improve a country's economic development. WID was adopted across donor organisations and NGOs and fed into the design of such project interventions as microcredit, education, and technology for the purpose of improving the status and livelihoods of women. Microcredit projects were often designed and implemented with a strong WID focus, especially by NGOs such as the Grameen Bank, which aimed to increase the productive roles of women. Although WID placed much-needed attention on the roles of women in development processes, it did not challenge existing gendered social structures or threaten fundamental change to male dominance and power. As a result women's projects were often promoted in isolation or as special-interest subprojects bolted onto traditional development interventions.

Though WID opened up some spaces for the women's agenda, it failed to bring women's issues onto the front page of development discourse. As it became obvious that women and men have to be involved in setting development goals and agendas, the shortcoming found in the WID approach led to a paradigm shift (i.e., the evolution of the gender and development approach [GAD]).

The WID approach was increasingly criticised because it did not attempt to change existing sociocultural gender biases. Furthermore, female-focused projects did not always result in improved economic conditions even for the women themselves. For example, most income-generating projects were found to be ineffective, and women-focused production/technology projects often added to rather than eased women's workloads and involved tradeoffs with other responsibilities. As a result, by the mid-1980s, GAD had emerged as the successor to WID with an underlying platform of explicitly challenging gender imbalances.

GAD addresses the needs and priorities of both women and men while analysing the outcomes of development based on such factors as gender, age, marital status, religion, ethnicity, and class. No longer are women (or men) treated as a homogenous group while the underlying structural inequalities in societies are treated as important variables shaping and reshaping women's and men's experiences in societies.

GAD, in contrast to WID, does not concentrate its attention exclusively on women but examines the social construction of gender and the assignment of specific roles, responsibilities, and expectations to women and men. The GAD approach aims to understand the power dynamics between men and women in different contexts, arguing it is only by understanding gender power relations that development can empower women and thereby create positive and sustainable socioeconomic change (Pettman 2004).

Despite the paradigm shift, women-empowerment and gender-equality principles continue to guide national development agendas. While gender equality remains an end in itself, the women-empowerment agenda remains an entry point in this process. Within the development praxis, gender equality remains a means to an end, i.e., sustainable human development. With the introduction of the Millennium Development Goals, there is now more vigorous global and national attention on gender-sensitive policies. The MDG 3, which aimed to achieve gender equality and women's empowerment, is not only of intrinsic value in itself but also central to the attainment of all other MDGs.

However, while feminist theory and practice over the last three decades and more has been systematically critiqued, reenvisioned, and reconstructed, little of the dynamic debate about race, class, imperialism, and other interrelated structural inequalities seems to have permeated the field of gender and development. Thus many of the prescriptions and practices associated with GAD continue to be underpinned with universalistic assumptions about women, men, and gender relations. GAD has served to domesticate dissent rather than to lend those women who would challenge the status quo the support with which to do it.

Challenging and potentially transforming existing relations of power as advocated by the GAD paradigm involves not only empowerment but also resistance: the two are inextricably intertwined. More often than not, this resistance runs directly counter to the neoliberal model, demanding the redistribution of resources, challenging the operation of markets, and organising against state repression. To conceive of empowerment in this way is to reveal the contradiction at the heart of neoliberal development's interventions in this field: for all the talk about empowerment, there are few development agencies that would be prepared to support women's mobilising in these ways. When women engage in struggles for transformation, they take part in a process of challenging and changing the very norms of behaviour that are reinforced by neoliberal development.

Challenging the Neoliberal Paradigms

Neoliberal models of market-led growth accompanied by certain economic and trade policy choices have proven to be problematic for much of the world's population, especially rural women and their communities. These policy choices assumes free trade, investment liberalization, private-sector and financial-system deregulation, and the privatization of public-owned enterprises and services would lead to sustained economic growth and improved productive capacities, all leading to increased employment opportunities, improved food security, and better lives overall. Yet the results of these policy choices—typically treated as gender neutral—have been mixed, with women and men impacted differently by the distribution of key economic and financial resources through markets and state interventions that are anything but gender neutral (United Nations 2009).

The rise of neoliberal policies over the last twenty-five years has resulted in the dominant rule of the market, greater openness to international trade and investment, reduced roles for governments, privatization, and a focus on individual rather than collective responsibility. The world is thus moving toward greater inequality and injustice within and among states as well as among women even while women in some settings are achieving a degree of equality with men.

In this setting of increasing worldwide inequality, the path toward gender equality becomes more difficult.

While neoliberal trade policies have tended toward the promotion of exports in recent decades, a number of factors, such as increased competition at the global market and the removal of tariffs and other trade taxes, have led to decreased revenue from international trade. At the same time, fiscal policies have focused on debt management and budget stabilization, resulting in reduced government spending and the adoption of increased user fees for essential rural infrastructure and public services (e.g., health care and social services). Limited or decreasing public budgets have made these services less accessible to women living in rural areas while increasing their burdens of unpaid care work and subsequently reducing their time to engage in economic activities. The result has been an increasing divide between those who can afford to pay for basic services and those who do not have the financial means to access them.

Neoliberal policies have given rise to what critics call a feminisation of labour accompanied by a deterioration of working conditions—casualisation, flexibilisation, violation of international labour standards, and low wages (Moghadam 2005). In addition the antipoverty programmes that have arisen in part to mitigate the effects of neoliberal economic reforms have a marked tendency to reproduce and reinforce deeply conservative notions of womanhood and of women's roles within the family (Molyneux 2006).

Using Nigeria as a specific example, the liberal economic policy pursued by the government had a lot of implications for rural women. For instance, the continuous withdrawal of real or imagined subsidies on petroleum products such as kerosene, which is generally used by rural women for domestic purposes, has caused them to become scarce commodities these women cannot easily afford. Many have resorted to the use of charcoal and firewood as alternatives for cooking. This has made women and young girls in the home spend more time and energy in search of firewood for cooking because coal cooking as an alternative is not only tedious but hazardous.

Actually the poverty-reduction strategies of the immediate past government of Olusegun Obasanjo (1999–2007), such as NEEDS 2004 (National Economic Empowerment Development Strategy) and SEEDS 2005 (State Economic Empowerment and Development Strategy), have not helped the situation of Nigerian women in rural areas as their implementation has been fraught with great challenges. The NEEDS/SEEDS document seems to view agricultural developments only from the agrobusiness point of view. There is no policy on how women can be empowered through agriculture; how farmers can define their own agricultural practices, which are ecological and culturally appropriate to their unique circumstances; or farmers' abilities to make informed choices, which are critical in the success of agriculture.

Most rural women workers are unpaid family workers or self-employed, typically in low-paying work (ILO 2009) as they seek to provide goods and services for both home consumption and for sale in local markets or peri-urban and urban markets. Moreover their time to engage in waged market opportunities is often limited compared to men's (FAO, IFAD, and ILO 2010). Rural women are often viewed as playing helping roles rather than as being active as farmers or employees in their own right.

The Africa Policy Environment and Gender-Responsive Governance

The gender-equality project has gained momentum in Africa as African countries have participated proactively in the various regional and international initiatives and events to promote gender equality since the 1995 Beijing International Conference on Women and the adoption of the Beijing Platforms for Action (BPFA). To implement these platforms, African leaders have put regional resolutions and mechanisms in place to translate their commitments into action: the Solemn Declaration on Gender Equality in Africa, adopted by African heads of state and government, which obliges states to respect normative standards of women's human rights; the protocol to the African Charter on Human and People's Rights on the Rights of Women in Africa; the gender parity of the Commission of the African Union; and the New Partnership for Africa's Development (NEPAD), endorsed in 2001 by African heads of state and government, which spells out gender equality as one of the core principles that underscore the new strategic vision for the long-term development of the continent.

The Protocol on the Rights of Women in Africa is a protocol to the African Charter on Human and People's Rights (ACHPR). The protocol, which was adopted on July 2003 in Maputo, reaffirmed African's commitment to the protection of women's rights as enshrined in major international instruments of human rights. The protocol endorses affirmative action to promote the equal participation of women, including equal representation in elected offices, and calls for the equal representation of women in the judiciary and law-enforcement agencies (African Union 2003). Furthermore the creation of the African Union, which is committed by its Constitutive Act to the principle of gender equality, provides further opportunities for institutionalizing gender mainstreaming and increased political participation by African women in regional decision making.

The Convention on the Elimination of All Forms of Discrimination against Women (CEDAW) and its optional protocol promote gender equality in access to social and economic opportunities and political power. As the first international treaty dealing explicitly with women's rights, it provides for the elimination of discrimination against women in particular in the political, social, economic, and cultural fields through a range of legal and policy interventions.

Despite the fact that most African governments have adopted international and regional instruments and resolutions that promote women's rights, African women still face institutional, legal, political, environmental, and socioeconomic constraints that impact their capacities and abilities to undertake sustainable livelihoods. These constraints have served to exclude women from recognized development benefits and opportunities—a phenomenon more pronounced among rural women, who are the backbone of the economy, constituting 70 percent of farm labour and producing 50 percent of food in Africa (Economic Commission for Africa 2009).

African governments have generally found that the mechanisms for the integration of gender equality and women's empowerment remain weak at all levels, lacking adequate capacity and funding. With line ministries unable to reach gender-equality targets owing to low levels of resource allocation and gender concerns being treated rhetorically or as separate women's projects, sex-disaggregated data and information from gender-sensitive indicators are often not collected, lost in the aggregation of published data, or not used.

Gender-Responsive Governance and Development

The relationship between governance, poverty reduction, and gender equality at the grassroots level is the key to sustainable development based on equality and equity and the effective participation of all stakeholders at all levels of society. A major concern in many African countries is continued women's exclusion at all levels, including grassroots, from important negotiations or their purely token representation without possibility for meaningful contribution. Women's as well as men's voices must be heard in all areas of development, including in analyses of poverty and the development of strategies and programmes. What has also emerged very clearly from research in Africa is that women at the grassroots level have an important contribution to make to the development of participatory forms of democracy. Facilitating women's participation can move institutions toward more-inclusive forms of democracy (Ashworth 1994).

Women's limited access to resources, public debate, and political decision making is still insufficiently considered in mainstream governance literature. Only 10 to 12 percent of parliamentarians worldwide are women. A major area of concern regarding gender equality and governance is thus the issue of women's participation. Equally important is the lack of attention to relevant gender perspectives in both process and substance. Governance policies are developed by institutions whose rules, norms, and practices often effectively restrict women's right to meaningful participation and their potential to make real choices. Gender perspectives are important in governance in particular because the discourse, procedures, structures, and functions of governance remain heavily skewed. This raises important questions about transparency, inclusion, legitimacy, and accountability—all of which lie at the heart of the governance debate.

In gender-responsive governance, there exists equality among women and men (access to resources, participation in decision making, sharing of benefits); respect for human rights; empowerment of women; and a transformative agenda. Its attainment through the preparation of a gender and development (GAD) plan and budget can be a potent advocacy tool and has its implications for social equity. The GAD plan and budget translate political commitments and goals into reality and reflect the government's social and economic priorities at various levels.

Governance must be gender sensitive if it is to be equitable, sustainable, and effective. Participation and civic engagement are critical determinants of good governance, a concept that addresses issues of social equity and political legitimacy and not merely the efficient management of infrastructure and services. The different ways in which women and men participate in and benefit from urban governance are significantly shaped by prevailing constructions of gender, whose norms, expectations, and institutional expressions constrain women's access to the social, economic, and political resources. Most societies ascribe roles and responsibilities to women and men differentially but fail to value or even account for the crucial contributions women's labour makes to household and community maintenance. Unfortunately such social reproduction allows little time (or, in some cases, permission) for women to participate in civic life in ways that help them determine their own lives (Boserup 1970).

Components of Gender-Responsive Governance

This section looks at the various components of gender-responsive governance and their implications for development agendas in Africa.

Women Empowerment and Poverty Eradication

Gender-responsive governance, gender equality, and women's empowerment are necessary conditions for the reduction of poverty. The importance of these factors is affirmed by numerous international human-rights and social-justice instruments. There is also a large body of evidence showing gender equality enhances good government and poverty reduction (Buvinic and King 2007; DFID 2007). Sustainable poverty reduction requires the full involvement of women as central actors in the processes of governance (Archer 1994)

Not only is poverty described as having a woman's face (FAO, IFAD, and ILO 2010; UNIFEM 2005; World Bank 2001), but the underlying determinants of poverty are traced to the subtle but enduring nature of gender inequalities at the levels of both policy and practice. The feminisation of poverty is heightened in both public and private engagements in Africa through non-gender-responsive methods of resource allocations, inequity in human resource development, low participation of women in decision making, and, most importantly, in politics and governance.

Gender Mainstreaming

"Gender mainstreaming is the multifaceted project of using gender analysis in addressing the mainstream agenda and of getting gender-related issues onto the mainstream agenda" (Ackerly 2004, 290).

A key strategy in promoting gender-responsive governance has been the adoption of gender mainstreaming tools that ensure women's and men's concerns and priorities are incorporated into development policies, strategies, and interventions at all levels and all stages including policy formulation and programme/project planning, implementation, monitoring, and evaluation.

Mainstreaming is not an end in itself but a strategy, an approach, a means to achieve the goal of gender equality. Mainstreaming involves ensuring that gender perspectives and attention to the goal of gender equality are central to all activities—policy development, research, advocacy/dialogue, legislation, resource allocation, planning, and implementation. According to the United Nations definition (ECOSOC 1997):

> Mainstreaming a gender perspective is the process of assessing the implications for women and men of any planned action, including legislation, policies or programmes, in all areas and at all levels. It is a strategy for making women's as well as men's concerns and experiences an integral dimension of the design, implementation, monitoring and evaluation of policies and programmes in all political, economic and societal spheres so that women and men can benefit equally and inequality is not perpetuated.

The need for gender mainstreaming is recognized as necessary for institutionalizing gender equity in governance and administrative structures at local, national, and international policymaking levels, and gender-mainstreaming strategies are on the agendas of many governments as well as multilateral and bilateral organizations as models of incremental social change (Ackerly 2004).

Gender mainstreaming (African Development Forum 2008) means:

- Forging and strengthening the political will to achieve gender equality and equity at the local, national, regional, and global levels.
- Incorporating a gender perspective into the planning processes of all ministries and departments of government, particularly those concerned with macroeconomic and development planning, personnel policies and management, and legal affairs.
- Integrating a gender perspective into all phases of sectoral planning cycles including analysis development, appraisal, implementation, monitoring and evaluation policies, programmes, and projects.
- Using sex-disaggregated data (data on men and women that is collected and presented separately) in statistical analysis to reveal how policies impact women and men differently.
- Increasing the numbers of women in decision-making positions in government and the private and public sectors.
- Providing tools and training in gender awareness, gender analysis, and gender planning to decision makers, senior managers, and other key personnel.

Women's Participation in Policy Decisions

What has been the quality of participation of women in decision making? Has women's participation made a difference in decision making? Although African countries have made some progress in women's representation in parliaments and ministries, it is important to note that this higher representation has not yet systematically led to adequate budgets, institutional frameworks, and policies for implementing gender programmes for gender equality (Economic Commission for Africa 2009). The major challenges affecting women's effective participation include illiteracy and lack of confidence that renders the women unable to articulate the issues effectively and make contributions; gender relations of power; and party politics. There is a clear need for building the capacity of women who are in politics in addition to those who hold promise as leaders through tailored training programmes, particularly in areas such as leadership skills, confidence building, networking, advocacy, and fundraising.

Increased participation of women in politics in most African countries is being achieved through constitution reviews, national gender policies, and strategies such as affirmative action and quota systems. Although some of these strategies (especially affirmative action) have been criticised, they remain very viable options in countries where politics bears a masculine face. As of 2006, six African countries had constitutional quotas, nineteen countries had voluntary quotas, and three had reserved-seats system (Okojie, Aina, and Akanji 2007). Quotas have proven to be an effective instrument for promoting gender equality in political representation when implemented with care. With quota provisions Rwanda has become the country with the highest female representation in parliament in the world. However, some authors argue that the extent to which the quota system translates to actual decision-making power for women is questionable; hence, in most cases, "quota provisions may be merely symbolic" (Dahlerup and Freidenvall 2005; Grown 2006).

Gender-Sensitive Economic Governance

Budgets influence the overall levels of national income and employment and reflect a government's political priorities regarding public investment. They are a powerful tool for promoting gender equality within national development frameworks. Gender budgeting aims to mainstream a gender-equality perspective into public finance by ensuring budgets are planned, approved, executed, monitored, and audited in a gender-sensitive way. This means policies are assessed in terms of their gender impacts, and budget allocations are made to reduce gender gaps. Gender budgeting ensures public investment choices address gender-related needs and helps monitor progress toward policy goals and commitments. By tracking how money is spent, gender budgeting increases accountability, transparency, and, in a larger sense, good economic governance. It also helps ensure governments are held accountable for international commitments they have made to women. More than sixty countries in the world are now practicing gender budgeting but only few in Africa.

Engendering the budget does not mean creating separate budgets for men and women (50/50), nor does it mean integrating only gender issues into the resource allocation (budget). Rather, engendering the budget is a holistic and strategic process that entails first looking at the policies through a gender lens and then scrutinizing the budget. It is based on the standpoint that the budget is an important tool and part of the overall planning process.

An analysis of the development policies adopted by African countries suggests they are based on conventional paradigms and models that overlook social dimensions in general and gender concerns in particular. Therefore, the first critical step in engendering the budget is to question the models and their derived policies, on which the budgets are based. There also is a need to mainstream gender into these strategies and policies/plans in order to engender their budgets. The process below should be followed (Diop 2002):

- Analyse from a gender perspective policies and programmes and their respective budgets.
- Formulate gender responsive budgets or adjust budgets to make them gender responsive, and implement them.
- Monitor and evaluate impacts on both men and women.
- Mainstream gender into the participatory poverty assessment (PPA).
- Women and men, girls and boys, should participate equally in the poverty assessment to voice how they perceive poverty, how it affects them, what their coping strategies are, and how they participate in poverty-reduction programmes.
- Mainstream gender into the poverty diagnosis and analysis. This consists of using the outcomes of the PPA backed up by gender-disaggregated data to document each poverty dimension from a gender perspective, e.g., lack of capabilities, lack of opportunities, vulnerability, disempowerment, etc.
- Use the outcome of the poverty diagnosis/analysis to inform elaboration of poverty priority areas for action.
- Formulate a gender-responsive budget to implement the poverty-reduction strategies, which consist of allocating resources to the gender-responsive priority areas for action.

Actors to Implement Gender-Responsive Governance

Gender-responsive governance depends on dynamic and active partnerships in the social and political fora that elaborate and redefine public policy.

Together these strategic partnerships can uphold the rights of citizens to participation, information, and accountability. They need to include civil society and especially women's networks at grassroots, local, national, and global levels. There is a need for all relevant stakeholders to focus more on and take concrete steps toward promoting gender equality in development since men and women experience political participation and are affected by poverty differently.

National Governments

Governments in Africa need to scale up the promotion of gender equality and women's empowerment through the enactment of relevant policies, legislation, and effective strategies. The past few decades in Africa have been characterized by the adoption of international and regional laws aimed at improving the status of women. However, the lack of accountability to honour commitments to gender equality, equity, and empowerment of women and girls, coupled with the prevalence of patriarchal systems, continues to prevent the translation of these policies and programmes into concrete actions that will positively impact the lives of African women.

Governments and policymakers must take concrete action to address poverty from a gender perspective based on integrating gender concerns in all programming and addressing specific issues that contribute to poverty-related gender disparities. Projects to improve the status of women must consider the different roles, needs, and perceptions of women and men. They must take into account the gender-based constraints women face, particularly the factors that limit their participation in development. Direct involvement of women through active participation in project planning, design, implementation, and evaluation empowers them and gives them a stronger sense of ownership and a more pronounced stake in project success. The governments must take responsibility for the following actions:

- Mobilization and sensitization of women for national politics at all spheres of government.

- Borrowing from best practices identified in this field, including:
  - o Engendering national budgets.
  - o Entrenching principles of gender equality in a country's constitution and other legal frameworks.
  - o Domesticating CEDAW and other treaties on gender equality.
  - o Imbibing a gender culture in the country, including a gendered language in all official documents.
  - o Enforcing all political parties to comply with gender-equality principles both in theory and practice and ensuring leadership of parties and constitutions reflect this.
- Promoting gender education at all levels—primary, secondary, and tertiary. This simply means textbooks and pedagogy are engendered across disciplines and the government invests in gender studies as a discipline.
- Supporting research and media programmes that propagate gender-equality values.
- Building the skills of female politicians in the area of fundraising.
- Working closely with traditional institutions, political parties, and the media to achieve gender equity in political participation and representation.
- Developing gender-disaggregated statistics to enable governments to cost services they provide and identify who is accessing them.
- Developing clear legislative frameworks for protecting the rights of women regarding inheritance of land and land-based resources and proactively informing women of their rights in this regard.
- Tackling the deeply rooted cultural norms and practices that underlie discrimination and prolong it at the community and household levels, even where legal frameworks that protect women's rights are in place.

Civil society organizations (CSOs), nongovernmental organizations (NGOs), and development partners must focus on:

- Building women's capacity to resist gender-based intimidating attitudes in party politics, etc. Therefore there is a need for more grassroots mobilisation and advocacy for female participation in politics, the economy, public life, etc.

- Targeting men as agents of change for women's empowerment and gender-equality agendas.
- Encouraging positive attitudes toward the "girl child" education at the household level.

Local communities must play important roles as drivers of change. Hence CSOs, NGOs, and even the government must target communities through a variety of methods.

CSOs and NGOs are best at mobilising for change at the grassroots level. They need to focus on the following areas of priorities:

- Mobilising community support for a gender equality the country's culture.
- Presenting through coalition efforts a unified front on gender equality with government and other interest groups.
- Capacity building in gender mainstreaming into policies, laws, and legislative processes for GEWE agendas to be functional.
- Providing support for grassroots mobilisation to enhance women's participation in politics.

Political parties would need to address the following areas:

- Restructuring all political parties and making them gender responsive.
- Demonstrating least the 30 percent affirmative action in party leadership and nomination of electoral candidates.

Development partners must focus on:

- Committing financial resources to support mechanisms-reform initiatives.
- Supporting monitoring and evaluation of land-reform processes to enhance women's access to and control of land.
- Supporting initiatives that provide financial support for the economic development of land owned by women.

- Encouraging gender-responsive budgeting in budget support.
- Reviving global efforts to recognize satellite accounts and provide resources to value and remunerate.
- Promoting the Paris Declaration and the Monterrey Consensus to include a focus on results and development policy goals for women and gender equality.
- Encouraging specific targets for gender in sector-wide approaches (SWAps) and establish budget-support mechanisms that encourage recipient countries to allocate money to the promotion of gender equality.
- Supporting the implementation of projects linked to gender equality, trade outcomes, and growth.
- Subsidising women's associations and providing free training to women managing associations.
- Supporting women employed in the agriculture sector to enhance their productive capacities.

Conclusion

This paper has argued that the quest for national growth and development, and the institutionalization of fundamental human rights and social justice in nation building, would remain elusive without consideration of the gender variable. Addressing governance and developmental issues (poverty reduction and corruption, notably) from a gender perspective presents a challenge to earlier development paradigms and brings broad-based benefits for all. Gender-responsive budgets, for example, provide a new and potentially effective mechanism for ensuring greater transparency and accountability in the allocation of public funds. The paper also recognized the importance of informed and constructive dialogue among all partners and identified a number of priority actions for future work: more data is needed, addressing both quantitative and qualitative dimensions and making full use of participatory action research, robust indicators and measures of progress on poverty reduction and political representation, and strengthened capabilities at both technical and political levels.

References

Ackerly, B. 2004. "Women's Human Rights Activists as Political Theorists" in L. Ricciutelli, A. R. Miles, and M. H. McFadden, eds. *Feminist Politics, Activism and Vision: local and global challenges.* London and New York: Zed Books/Inanna.

African Development Forum. 2008. "Action on gender equality, empowerment and ending violence against women in Africa." Sixth African Development Forum, Addis Ababa, Ethiopia, November 19–21.

Africa Partnership Forum. 2007. "Gender and Economic Empowerment in Africa." 8th Meeting of the Africa Partnership Forum, Berlin, Germany.

African Union. 2003. "Protocol to the African Charter on Human and Peoples' Rights on the Rights of Women in Africa." General Assembly of the African Union, Maputo, Mozambique, July.

Aina, O.I. 2008. "The Gender Equality / Women Empowerment (GEWE) Agenda and the Nigerian Development." Paper presented at the International Laboratory for PhD Students on Globalisation, Social Problems and Social Policy, Maiduguri, Nigeria, November 18–23.

Aina, O.I. and Olayode, K.O. 2011 "Gender equality and Women empowerment in a Democratising Society: Issues and Challenges." Paper presented at the 16th Annual Conference of ASAN: Ilorin, Kwara State.

Archer, R. 1994. *Markets and Good Government: The Way Forward for Economic and Social Development?* Geneva: UN Non-Government Liaison Service.

Ashworth, G. 1994 *Women, Public Life and Governance.* Geneva, UN Economic Commission for Europe.

Boserup, E. 1970 *Women's Role in Economic Development*. London: George Allen and Unwin.

Buvinic, M. and King, E.M. "Smart Economics." *Finance and Development* 44, 2 (2007): 7–12.

Dahlerup, D. and Freidenvall, L. "Quotas as a 'Fast Track' to Equal Representation of Women: Why Scandinavia is No Longer the Model." *International Feminist Journal of Politics* 7, 1 (2005): 26–48.

DFID. 2007. *Gender Equality at the Heart of Development*. Accessed December 11, 2012. http://webarchive.nationalarchives.gov.uk/+/http:/www.dfid.gov.uk/Documents/publications/gender-equality.pdf

Diop, N. 2002. "Translating Government's Commitment into actions. The Rwanda Gender Budgeting Initiative" in D. Budlender and G. Hewitt. *Gender Budgets Make More Cents*. The Commonwealth Secretariat.

Economic Commission for Africa. 2009. *Compendium of Emerging Good Practices in Gender Mainstreaming*. Addis Ababa: African Centre for Gender and Social Development.

ECOSOC. 1997. "Report of the Economic and Social Council for 1997." Accessed May 2013. http://www.un.org/documents/ga/docs/52/plenary/a52-3.htm.

Unspecified. 1992. *Panorama. Statistical Data Concerning the Participation of Women in political and public decision-making*. V/5145/93-FR/EN. [EU Commission— Working Document].

FAO, IFAD, and ILO. 2010. *Gender Dimensions of Agricultural and rural Employment: Differentiated Pathways out of poverty: status, trends and gaps*. Rome: Food and Agricultural Organization/International Fund for Agricultural Development/International Labour Organization.

González, M.J., Jurado,T., and Naldini, M. 2000. *Gender Inequalities in Southern Europe: Women,Work andWelfare in the 1990s.* London and Portland: Frank Cass Publishers.

Grown, C. 2006. "Indicators and Indices of Gender Equality: What Do They Measure and What Do They Miss?" Background paper for *Global Monitoring Report 2007*, Washington D.C.: World Bank.

ILO. 2009. *Global Employment Trends for Women.* Geneva: International Labour Organization.

March, C., Smyth, I., and Mukhopadhyay, M. 1999. *A Guide to Gender-Analysis Frameworks.* England: Oxfam.

Martinussen, J. 1997. *State, Society and Markets: A Guide to Competing Theories of Development.* London and New York: Zed Books.

Moghadam, V.M. 2005. *Globalizing Women: Transnational Feminist Networks.* Baltimore: Johns Hopkins University Press.

Molyneux, M. "Mothers at the Service of the New Poverty Agenda: Progresa/ Oportunidades, Mexico's Conditional Transfer Programme." *Social Policy and Administration* 40, 4 (2006): 425–49.

Okojie, C., Aina, O. I., and Akanji, B. 2007. "Tools and Guidelines for Mainstreaming Gender into Budget Process: A Handbook for Policymakers." Unpublished.

Olayode, K.O. 2011. "MDGs and African-EU Strategic Partnership" in A. Sesay and O. C. Eze, eds. *African Union and European Union Strategic Partnership.* Lagos: Nigeria Institute of International Affairs.

Pettman, J.J. 2004. "Global Politics and Transnational Feminisms" in L. Ricciutelli, A. R. Miles, and M.H. McFadden, eds. *Feminist Politics, Activism and Vision.* London and New York: Zed Books/Inanna.

Sen, G. and Grown, C.A. 1988. *Development, Crises and Alternative Visions. Third World Women's Perspectives.* London and USA: Earthscan/Monthly Review Press.

United Nations. 2009. *World Survey on the Role of Women in Development. Women's Control over Economic Resources and Access to Financial Resources including Microfinance.* Accessed May 2013. http://www.un.org/womenwatch/daw/ws2009/.

UNDP. 2008. *Human Development Report 2007/8. Fighting climate change: Human solidarity in a divided world.* New York: UNDP.

UNDP. 1995. *Human Development Report 1995. Gender and Human Development.* New York: UNDP.

UNIFEM. 2005. *Progress of World Women Report: Women, Work and Poverty.* New York: UNIFEM.

World Bank. 2002. *Ghana Strategic Country Gender Assessment. Briefing Note for the Ghana Poverty Reduction Strategy.* New York: World Bank.

World Bank. 2001. *Engendering Development through Gender Equality in Rights, Resources and Voice.* New York: Oxford University Press and World Bank.

World Bank. 2000. *Evaluating the Gender Impact of Bank Assistance.* Washington, DC: World Bank.

CHAPTER 5

LOST IN THE WOODS: REFLECTIONS ON EARLY TWENTY-FIRST-CENTURY NIGERIAN SOCIAL MOVEMENTS

Ike Okonta

How can they say we are finished
We have just begun
When we have nowhere else to run to
We have nowhere else to go
    —TY Bello, Nigerian singer, "The Future"

Two bombs went off in the afternoon of October 1, 2010, in Abuja, the Nigerian capital, as political leaders and their foreign guests were celebrating the fiftieth anniversary of the country's independence. Eagle Square, the expansive official pavilion in the centre of the city where President Goodluck Jonathan and the other worthies were seated, was spared. But citizens who had gathered in the adjoining streets to participate in the event were not so lucky. Several, including little children, were instantly killed. Many more were seriously injured.

The attack, blamed on the Movement for the Emancipation of the Niger Delta (MEND), a violent ethnic militia that had emerged in Nigeria's oil-producing region in January 2006, not only demonstrated the militia's ability to reach beyond its main operational base in the southern tip of the country to strike targets in the capital; it also underlined the profound rage of the younger generation of Nigerians at a political system that had reduced them to the status of impoverished second-class citizens since formal military dictatorship had ended in May 1999. But the Abuja bombings had a deeper significance. The bloody event underlined yet another shift in the rules of political engagement from nonviolent civic protest to the trench warfare that had marked the turbulent 1960s, culminating in the thirty-month-long civil war of 1967–70—a violent politics ordinary Nigerians thought they had left behind forever when the guns had stopped firing in January 1970.

Like a good part of Africa, Nigeria faced three key challenges as economic growth and broad citizen prosperity began to stall in the early 1980s, following the contagion of deep financial crisis in the United States and Western Europe. Military dictatorship, which had temporarily ended in 1979, had returned four years later when it became clear the politicians were clueless about what policies to adopt to bring the country out of financial ruin. Citizens who had clamoured for a return to democratic rule since the end of the civil war in 1970 still wanted to participate in governance but did not know how to go about this following the perfidy and massive corruption that had characterized the Second Republic the soldiers had just displaced.

Second, the Nigerian military junta, led by General Ibrahim Babangida from August 1985 onward, had adopted an IMF-inspired structural adjustment programme (SAP) that, in a doomed effort to revive the comatose economy, devalued the currency, savagely cut social subsidies, and, borrowing from Prime Minister Margaret Thatcher in Great Britain, vigorously pursued a programme of privatizing public corporations and downsizing the civil service. The instant effect was an explosion in unemployment, growing poverty, and the widely shared feeling among youth, the poor, and the unemployed that the Nigerian state had been taken over by a particularly vicious faction of the elite and their foreign collaborators, all intent on destroying the social and economic bases of their continued existence.

Third, the evident inability or refusal of the state to address the pressing social and economic needs of the vulnerable triggered the resurgence of ethnic nationalism and other primordial tendencies, leading civic leaders and other political actors opposed to the military government to begin to call for the convocation of a sovereign national conference where, in their own words, "the national question" would be addressed. There was even talk of a second civil war.

Further elaboration of these three main problems, even as the repressive military junta increasingly tightened its grip on power in the early 1990s, created fertile soil for the emergence of powerful social movements committed to ending military dictatorship and bringing about a democratically elected government that would put an end to official corruption and return the country to the path of shared prosperity.

This chapter examines the emergence, character, and trajectory of three of these movements against wider social and political developments in the country from the 1980s to the present. Campaign for Democracy (CD) is a coalition of several pro-democracy and human-rights organizations that was created in 1991 as the popular demand for an end to military rule reached a crescendo. The Movement for the Emancipation of the Niger Delta (MEND) announced its emergence with a series of bloody attacks on the facilities of Shell Producing Development Company (SPDC), the leading international oil company operating in the Niger Delta, in January 2006. The militia's advertised goal is to force officials in Abuja to cede the majority share of the oil receipts, still controlled by the federal government, to the impoverished local communities in the delta region where the oil is produced. Save Nigeria Group (SNG) entered the turbulent terrain of national politics in January 2010 as a powerful cabal composed mainly of cabinet ministers, National Assembly members, and political advisers loyal to ailing President Umaru Musa Yar'Adua, who had been flown to Saudi Arabia for medical attention but refused to hand over power temporarily to the vice president as stipulated by the Constitution. SNG, riding the crest of popular demand that the provisions of the constitution be immediately implemented, emerged to break the deadlock.

The central question this article grapples with is why, with Africa's economic and social condition taking a turn for the worse in the first decade of the twenty-first century in the wake of disastrous structural adjustment, progressive Nigerian social movements, the above-mentioned three in particular, have failed to make the all-important transition to become organizations seriously focused on the question of political power and how it might be fruitfully utilized to address the country's burgeoning problems. Even if it were argued that these movements were in actuality pressure groups with the limited goals of ending military rule and, following the return of democratic government, campaigning for accountability and equitable allocation of public resources, these modest objectives have not been achieved either. Indeed thirteen years after the return of civil government, the ruling Peoples' Democratic Party (PDP) is as entrenched in power as ever after successfully rigging elections in 1999, 2003, 2007, and 2011. A large swathe of the social movements and NGOs that made appearances in the 1980s and the early 1990s have either gone extinct or become comatose and ineffective. Where they still exist, their strategies are incoherent, self-serving, or a combination of these. What specific social, economic, and political forces are at work shaping the trajectory and eventual impotence of these movements? How might these forces be fruitfully engaged to birth a renaissance of social movements in Nigeria to actively challenge an increasingly authoritarian and rapine state and indeed mobilize the broad citizenry behind a project of social emancipation and progressive and accountable government?

I trace in a second section the return of military dictatorship in the country in the early 1980s and the way the harsh social and economic policies the generals pursued triggered the emergence of these social movements. I also examine the goals they set for themselves and the conditions that shaped the adoption of these goals. The third section examines in detail these social movements, the social and economic forces that shaped this character, their analyses of Nigeria's fundamental problems, and how this informed the strategies they adopted in their struggles with the state. In the fourth section, I examine why these movements failed to achieve the three central goals of democracy and the rule of law, a prosperous economy in which all citizens would have a meaningful share, and a united country founded on and animated by civic ideals.

Historically Lagos, the country's most populous and cosmopolitan city, functioned as the base of civic nationalists battling British colonialism and, subsequently, indigenous military dictatorship. The city was Nigeria's answer to the state of Piedmont in the era of Italy's *Risorgimento*. Following the return to civil rule in 1999, the city and the region of which it is part was taken over by a political party that espoused an ethno-regional agenda, effectively shutting out civic actors from other ethnic groups who came of age politically in the 1980s, seeing Lagos as the great city on a hill from which to do battle with the forces impeding Nigeria's progress. This section also analyses the profound consequences of this ethnic narrowing of the political terrain in the city for progressive civic movements and the way this development, among several others, have continued to thwart efforts at reinvigorating the project of social and political emancipation in the country.

Concluding, I attempt to project into the future, looking at the likely trajectory of the country's worsening political and economic crises and the ways in which increasingly desperate citizens and inchoate early twenty-first-century social movements might be regalvanized to overcome local and international environments that are currently hostile to a progressive social project founded on equity and shared prosperity.

Challenging the Man on Horseback

Since January 1966, when the Nigerian armed forces put an end to the elected First Republic through a bloody coup, political and intellectual elites have always considered the latter as interlopers in the political arena—a necessary evil to be tolerated temporarily in times of profound political crisis. The unspoken understanding was that the soldiers would relinquish power and return to the barracks after they had taken the necessary corrective measures to reestablish political order. The forced reincorporation of secessionist Biafra in January following the end of a bloody thirty-month civil war and the oil boom that subsequently followed enabled the military junta that emerged from the political debris of the turbulent 1960s to project successfully the image of the brave man on horseback riding out to rescue a citizenry in distress—a Nigerian de Gaulle benevolently looking after the interests of the poor and socially excluded even as he used his gun to do battle with the forces working to undermine the unity and stability of the republic.

Moderate economic growth in the 1970s, powered by burgeoning oil receipts and a pragmatic development strategy that combined elements of social democracy and the free market to expand urban employment and the provision of social services, created a relatively content middle class (Forrest 1995). While poverty remained rife in rural areas, particularly as social spending was focused on the burgeoning cities, peasants and petty artisans were unable to organize politically to challenge the military junta and articulate their interests. The military junta, led by General Olusegun Obasanjo following the assassination of his principal in February 1976, handed over power to an elected government in October 1979. The politicians of the Second Republic, with the ruling National Party of Nigeria (NPN) in the lead, embarked on a programme of looting the treasury on assuming office. There was also massive capital flight in this period. The onset of economic difficulties in Western countries in the early 1980s led to a sharp drop in the price of oil, Nigeria's main export, which at that time accounted for 90 percent of export earnings. The country slid into economic recession in 1982.

The armed forces, led by General Muhammadu Buhari, ended the Second Republic in December 1983 and reestablished military rule. The massive corruption that flourished while the NPN was in power, and the inability of the politicians to return the country to the path of prosperity, had discredited the latter in the eyes of the citizenry, providing Buhari's government temporary breathing space (Falola and Ihonvbere 1985). He took draconian measures to curb corruption, balance the budget, and regalvanize economic growth. The government also rejected the International Monetary Fund's demand that the Naira be devalued and subsidies on social services and locally refined petroleum products be removed as a condition for a $2.8 billion loan. The economy began a slow and painful journey toward stabilization. Even so, the urban middle classes, long used to cheap imported luxuries, began to protest as the military government's policies restricted imports to machine parts and other necessities. The harsh decrees the government enacted to rein in growing public dissent and ensure that the ousted politicians remained in detention provided General Ibrahim Babangida, Buhari's chief of army staff, an opportunity to mount a palace coup and replace his boss in August 1985.

Adebayo Olukoshi, the Nigerian thinker and academic has observed, rightly in my view:

> At no time in Nigeria's postcolonial history has there been so massive an efflorescence of nonprofessional civil associations dedicated to the pursuit of democracy and the rule of law as in the period since 1986—following the introduction, by the government of General Ibrahim Babangida, of an International Monetary Fund/World Bank-sponsored Structural Adjustment Programme (SAP). (Olukoshi 1997, 379)

The last time the country experienced a similar civic flowering was in the immediate post-World War II period, when a myriad of civil and professional associations emerged and joined the nationalist struggle to win independence from British colonial rule. On seizing power General Babangida adopted an economic programme, drafted by the World Bank resident in the country, that massively devalued the currency, cut subsidies on petroleum products and social services, and dismantled trade and tariff policies that protected the country's nascent industrial sector. This neoliberal regime, a vital cog in the structural adjustment programme the IMF was implementing all over Africa at the time, was a radical departure from the mixed-economy consensus forged by Nigeria's leaders in the early 1960s. Babangida promised Nigerians these measures would be temporary, and the pain induced was designed to "rationalize" the economy and return the country to the prosperity the citizenry had enjoyed in the booming 1970s. The general also unfolded a new political programme in the same period that, he promised, would speedily return the country to democratic rule. Government officials claimed that economic liberalization would create a new class of prosperous economic actors who would support the political liberalization programme Babangida was pursuing, putting to rest the spectre of military intrusion in the country's politics for good.

By the early 1990s, not a single one of these promises had been kept. As the Naira continued its free fall, eroding the purchasing power of the middle classes, and as factories unable to import vital parts closed down, leading to a precipitate rise in unemployment, anti-SAP protests broke out in several parts of the country. The military government had banned an influential segment of the political class from participating in the new political transition programme and followed this up in October 1989 with imposing two new government-controlled political parties—the Social Democratic Party (SDP) and the National Republican Convention (NRC)—on the citizenry. The constitutions and policy platforms of the two parties, one a little to the left and the other a little to the right, were written by regime officials.

The central argument developed here is that citizens' resistance to a harsh economic programme that failed to yield tangible dividends and a political programme that disenfranchised them and repeatedly thwarted their demand for democratic government—authoritarian measures that were retained following the return of civilian rule in 1999—provided and continue to provide fertile soil for the emergence of powerful social movements in the country. The return of democracy and the rule of law, a growing and prosperous economy in which all would have an equitable share, and a united nation where ethnic and religious differences further accentuated by failed neoliberal economic policies would have no place were the three main tasks these social movements gave themselves. I argue they have so far failed to secure these goals because their strategies have not been informed by an understanding of the nature of power in the country and the way in which it deploys its social and economic guises to deflect resistance to its project. I examine three of these social movements—Campaign for Democracy (CD), MEND, and SNG—in detail in the next section.

Three Social Movements, or How to Walk in an Unrelenting Circle

Nigeria's social and economic crises predated General Babangida. In 1987, two years after he had seized power, income from oil exports was only $6 billion, a precipitate drop from a high of $26 billion in 1981. It rose to about $13 billion in 1990 but went down to $10 billion a year later. What galvanized public anger against SAP and the junta was, however, the authoritarian manner with which the economic programme was imposed, the lack of accountability in governance, and growing corruption linked to Babangida and other ranking military officers. Even worse, the years of fiscal discipline had neither diversified the economy from near-absolute dependence on oil nor generated the new jobs an increasingly impoverished citizenry needed.

In November 1991 several civil and professional associations that had led the struggle for democratization and respect for human rights following the advent of SAP in 1986 came together and established the Campaign for Democracy (CD), an umbrella organization (Olukoshi 1997, 380). Prominent among these associations were the Civil Liberties Organization (CLO), the country's first civil rights NGO; Committee for the Defence of Human Rights (CDHR); Constitutional Rights Project (CRP); Nigerian Union of Journalists (NUJ); Academic Staff Union of Nigerian Universities (ASUU); National Association of Nigerian Students (NANS), Nigerian Labour Congress (NLC); Nigerian Bar Association (NBA); Women in Nigeria; National Association of Democratic Lawyers (NADL); Nigerian Tenants Association (NTA); and Nigerian Medical Association (NMA). By 1990, four years after the inauguration of the junta's political transition programme, it had become obvious that General Babangida was reluctant to return the country to democratic rule. Campaign for Democracy set for itself the main goal of mobilizing the citizenry to demand free and fair elections, a process that would ultimately end with the armed forces quitting power. Front organizations financed by the government and designed to infiltrate civil society with pro-junta ideas and policies had also emerged in this period, and CD set out to combat them also.

Announcing his plan to establish two new junta-sponsored political parties and the determination of his government to ensure that the older generation politicians did not hijack the process in October 1989, General Babangida stated: "When we said new social order, 'new breed politicians' we meant business. We meant new political institutions with a new leadership group, not old political wolves in new breed sheep skins" (*African Guardian* 1989). The head of the junta was true to his word. He and his lieutenants not only closely orchestrated the emergence and development of the SDP and NRC, they were careful to exclude from these two parties politicians, pro-democracy activists, and labour leaders they knew would stoutly challenge their project of imposing on the country a "democracy" entirely devoid of civil and political liberties. The rapid growth of CD as a powerful social movement was because it offered the former a platform through which to participate in the unfolding political process even as the junta insisted they were undesirable elements.

Beko Ransome-Kuti, an influential medical doctor and president of the Committee for the Defence of Human Rights, served as CD's chairman. Ubani Chima, a charismatic pro-democracy activist who had cut his teeth as a student-union leader in the 1980s, was general secretary. CD also had offices in key cities all over the country manned by regional secretaries. As local, state, and national assembly elections were held in 1991 and 1992, CD officials dismissed the process leading to these elections as lacking in credibility, also arguing that the programmes and party manifestoes of the SDP and NRC did not sufficiently address the political and economic crises in which the country was mired. Indeed pro-democracy leaders had joined retired senior civil servants and technocrats in 1990 to call for a national conference where such contentious issues as the federal structure of the country, revenue allocation, and citizenship rights—referred to in popular parlance as "the national question"—would be debated openly. A date for the conference, to be held in Lagos, was fixed. Following threats from the government, the retired civil servants withdrew, but pro-democracy leaders pressed on, insisting the immediate convocation of a sovereign national conference that would address the national question and pave the way for free and fair elections was their minimum demand.

The annulment of the result of the presidential election held in June 1993—in which Moshood Abiola, a wealthy businessman, won on the platform of the SDP—threw the country into deep turmoil. Not only were pro-democracy campaigners and ordinary citizens outraged, but large swathes of the hitherto supine political class, now realizing the junta was determined to perpetuate itself in power, began to kick. General Babangida's attempts to muzzle an increasingly hostile press with military decrees only forced some of them—the most popular and widely read—underground (Dare 2007, 79–84).

Tapping the cocktail of widespread poverty, disgust with a corrupt military junta intent on frustrating citizens' demands for democracy and the rule of law, and a guerrilla press further amplifying this climate of anomie, CD, under the leadership of Beko Ransome-Kuti, began to mobilize the populace. The organization's goal during this period was to make the country ungovernable and compel the junta to reverse the cancellation of the June 1993 election. From June through October 1993, strikes, public demonstrations, and sometimes direct confrontations with the police and armed soldiers were organized, effectively paralyzing economic and social life in the cities. While the junta struck back, killing, jailing, and brutalizing several leaders of the pro-democracy movement, this tactic, instead of achieving the intended effect, transformed CD into the potent spearhead of a powerful countrywide social movement demanding democratic rule and social justice.

In November 1993 General Sani Abacha, Babangida's second in command, displaced the interim transitional government the latter had hastily cobbled together before relinquishing power the previous August. At this point the CD made the first fatal mistake. All the strands of the evidence have not yet come in, but there are strong indications that a faction of the umbrella organization collaborated with a section of the political class to facilitate Abacha's coup, having reached an agreement with the general's henchmen that the latter would rule only for a short period before handing power over to Abiola, winner of the June 1993 election. Abacha, on seizing power, not only reneged on this agreement but intensified the harassment of CD members and politicians, particularly those from the southwest region from where Abiola had come.

As the first anniversary of the 1993 presidential election annulment neared, a bitter but emboldened Abiola, returning from participating in Nelson Mandela's presidential inauguration ceremony, helped regalvanize the struggle to claim his mandate (*Thisday* 2012). The National Democratic Coalition (NADECO), a platform composed mainly of aggrieved southwest politicians, emerged shortly after, and its activities increasingly began to draw the attention of the media, to the detriment of CD. The establishment in November 1994of the Democratic Alternative (DA), a left-of-centre political party, by such leading CD stalwarts as Bamidele Aturu and Chima Ubani further deprived the umbrella organization of the mobilisation skills of these individuals. The rump of CD, instead of rallying behind DA as its political-party platform and alerting Nigerians to the strategic threat NADECO, with its narrow social base and vague programme, represented, did neither. This was the second fatal mistake.

Holly Burkhalter summed up the disintegration of the progressive forces that had temporarily overcome ethnic and religious barriers to demand for the return of democratic rule thus:

> The tragedy of the present crisis is that Nigerian citizens, who in the election seemed to have overcome a legacy of ethnic conflict by crossing ethnic and regional barriers to vote for Mr Abiola, have been forced once again to narrow their sights and put their ethnic identities first, rather than their citizenship as Nigerians. (Burkhalter 1993)

CD was the chief victim of this narrowing and ethnicisation of the political space, enabling government front groups and self-serving ethnic entrepreneurs to penetrate civil society and shore up military dictatorship under General Abacha.

Even with the death of Abacha and Abiola in quick succession in 1998, when it became increasingly clear that a now-discredited junta was working out a way to cede power, CD and other affiliate organizations were unable to seize the moment and mobilize the citizenry behind DA or another political party espousing progressive social policies. Thabo Mbeki, deputy president of South Africa and a veteran of the anti-apartheid struggle, visited Lagos in 1998 as political parties were being established and urged CD leaders—including Gani Fawehinmi, icon of the nation's human-rights struggle; Beko Kuti; and Olisa Agbakoba—to mobilize the pro-democracy movement behind a party that would contest the elections. An influential faction of CD, led by Fawehinmi, refused, insisting a temporary government of national unity that would convoke a sovereign national conference was their minimum demand. Explained Agbakoba, a lawyer and founder of the Civil Liberties Organization (CLO), Nigeria's premier human rights NGO:

> Gani's view was that unless we resolved what he called the GNU (Government of National Unity) and the Sovereign National Conference issue, we should not take part. Today, I am not sure that was right....I think that has proved to be a costly error because by 2003 when we decided to now come out, the party

that was going to be the party of the human rights community as AD (Alliance for Democracy) had been taken over. And there was no other platform…. (*The Sun* 2012)

This was CD's third fatal mistake.

The Peoples Democratic Party (PDP), sponsored by the departing junta, became the governing party after elections in April 1999 that were widely condemned by local and international observers, including President Jimmy Carter of the Carter Center, as replete with irregularities. Two other major parties also contested. Alliance for Democracy (AD), claiming a progressive platform, nevertheless adopted a political strategy that relied on its main ethnic base in the southwest of the country. All Peoples Party (later renamed All Nigeria Peoples Party), the platform of the late General Abacha's loyalists, also had a sectional base in the North. As PDP consolidated in subsequent elections, relying on financial inducement and sometimes outright violence to retain power in the federal centre and the majority of the states, opposition parties and social movements alike were exiled to the margins of political life. CD, while still plodding on, is now a pale shadow of its old self, unable to mobilize the millions of Nigerian citizens as it once did in the turbulent 1990s.

Movement for the Emancipation of the Niger Delta (MEND)

MEND is the violent, angry child of the aborted democratic promise in the Nigeria of the 1990s, enabling resurgent ethnic organizations and political parties allied to them to occupy the political space increasingly. Attahiru Jega has traced the beginnings of this form of exclusivist identity politics in post-civil-war Nigeria to the introduction of the structural adjustment programme in the 1980s, to the extent that the state, which historically has always played a commanding role in the control and distribution of strategic resources to favoured individuals and groups, found itself increasingly unable to fulfil this function. This development triggered an inter-elite struggle for both these shrinking resources and the state itself. According to Jega (2000, 19):

The ruling class derived both its origin and wealth from the state, around which it gravitates, using every available means to secure power and access. Hence, in the competition and struggle for state power, especially in the period of economic crisis, identity politics becomes heightened and tend to assume primacy.

MEND, a youth-led militia, announced its emergence on the Nigerian political scene with a spate of bombings in November 2005 through January 2006, targeting the installations of Shell Producing Development Company (SPDC), the local arm of the international oil company, and other oil majors operating in the Niger Delta, Nigeria's oil belt. The militia claimed that its chief grievance was that the bulk of the revenue derived from the Niger Delta oil fields, its home region, was controlled by the central government in Abuja, which was dominated by politicians from the major ethnic groups. MEND derived its base membership and leading commanders from the Ijaw, one of the prominent ethnic groups in the delta. The militia also rightly pointed out that oil production had destroyed the farmlands and rivers on which local people in the region relied for sustenance and called for a new political and economic arrangement in Nigeria giving primacy to fiscal federalism, thus enabling the ethnic groups in the delta region to control their natural resource endowments (Okonta 2006).

On first reading the press statements MEND spokespeople regularly put out on the Internet would appear to be informed by pan-ethnic considerations, the propaganda arm of yet another regionally based faction of the Nigerian ruling class that has, in anger and desperation, resorted to violence to press its claims on the state. But the militia's origin, membership, and modus operandi speak of far more complex economic and political developments, local and national, coming together to drive a social movement robustly civic at inception into an ethnic cul-de sac. MEND and the Movement for the Survival of the Ogoni People (MOSOP), founded by writer and minority-rights activist Ken Saro-Wiwa in 1990, are two sides of the same political coin—one angry and violent, the latter calm and peaceful but just as determined to secure justice for the impoverished local communities in the oil belt. Indeed the broad social movement for social justice in the region was triggered by MOSOP officials following the 1990 publication of the Ogoni Bill of Rights, in which they detailed a long list of grievances against the Nigerian state and the oil companies and called on other

Nigerians and the international community to join them in the project of birthing a new Nigeria founded on federalism, ethnic equality, and equity. It is not a coincidence that MOSOP emerged in the land of the Ogoni, one of the delta region's smaller ethnic groups, at a time when poverty and inter-ethnic discord had increased in the country, and it was clear to the discerning that SAP held no answers to Nigeria's mounting problems.

Following the hanging of Ken Saro-Wiwa and eight other members of MOSOP by the Abacha junta in November 1995 and the subsequent violent suppression of the organization, a spate of self-determination groups emerged in the region, espousing a mix of civic and ethnic goals. In Ijawland the more prominent of these youth-led groups coalesced to form the Ijaw Youth Council (IYC) in late 1998, on the eve of the military junta's disengagement from power following the deaths, in quick succession, of General Abacha and Moshood Abiola, winner of the 1993 presidential election—the latter while still in detention and under military guard. Led by Oronto Douglas, a charismatic lawyer and environmental-rights campaigner, and Asume Isaac Osuoka, a powerful orator and former student leader, IYC quickly became a significant force in the burgeoning campaign to curb the excesses of the Nigerian state and the oil companies. IYC published the Kaiama Declaration, a stirring narrative of the Ijaw people's ordeals in a Nigeria hijacked by a self-serving power elite and ending with a re-echoing of the Ogoni Bill of Rights' call for a sovereign national conference that would pave the way for democracy, social justice, and a new Nigerian federation of ethnic equals (Ijaw Youth Council 1998).

IYC was visited with brutal suppression by the military junta even as elections were being held to usher in Nigeria's Fourth Republic. President Jimmy Carter, under the auspices of the Atlanta-based Carter Center, monitored the presidential election in several parts of the delta region in April 1999 and turned in a damning report that highlighted poll rigging and other violations. The Peoples Democratic Party (PDP), blatantly favoured by the departing generals, took power in the federal centre and the majority of the states, including the key delta states of Rivers, Delta, and Bayelsa. However, as President Olusegun Obasanjo settled in to govern, the violent tactics the PDP governors employed in the delta states began to come home to roost. These PDP politicians, whose records of public service were virtually nonexistent, understood they had no chance of winning in a fair and free electoral context. Consequently they induced fringe members of the IYC and the other youth-led organizations with cash and promises of political office, armed them with guns and other lethal weapons, and used them to overawe their opponents and muscle themselves into power.

By 2005, two years after the PDP had "won" a second term deploying a mix of cash, intimidation, and outright violence, the PDP governors in the delta had returned the region to virtual military dictatorship where vote rigging, corruption, and widespread poverty proliferated. IYC, assailed by repression and financial inducement orchestrated by the state governors and their principals in Abuja, had splintered. Several other youth groups had reverted to ethnic jingoism and banditry, working as guns for hire in the governors' vigilant outfits—armed enforcers in the growing "bunkering" (oil-theft) industry—and kidnapping oil-company personnel to generate income. Their leaders saw themselves as the Nigerian equivalents of the warlords in crisis-torn Liberia and Sierra Leone in the 1990s and their followers as militants.

Even so it must be stated that these "warlords" exhibited complex split personalities, mixing thuggish behaviour and genuine concern for the plight of their afflicted land and its impoverished people. It was this stew of deepening poverty, banditry, patriotism, political authoritarianism, and ethnic populism, cynically parlayed by the governors even as they raided the public treasury with impunity, that gave birth to MEND. The immediate trigger was the incarceration of the governor of Bayelsa state, who was styled as the governor general of the Ijaw nation by President Obasanjo in mid-2005 for corruptly enriching himself. Claiming that the Ijaw people and the Niger delta region of which they are part had been severely wounded, several of these warlords banded together, established MEND as a loose coalition of militant organizations, and proceeded on a violent campaign against the state and the oil companies that, they said, were eating all the oil and leaving only environmental carnage for the local people.

While MEND drew inspiration and intellectual guidance from the campaign of the environmental and pro-democracy organizations in Port Harcourt and other delta cities that remained true to the civic concerns that animated their work, the two broad groups were unable to integrate or even reach agreement on a common strategy. Many civic, youth, and community leaders, while assert-ing that MEND had legitimate grievances, openly condemned the militia's vio-lent methods and urged its leaders to lay down their arms and dialogue with the central government on ways in which these grievances could be addressed. The devastating effect of MEND's attacks on oil installations, leading to a sharp drop in production and a concomitant price hike in the international market, also led concerned energy importers like the United States to begin the process of quietly working out a strategy to contain the growing insurgency in Nigeria's oil region. The general elections of 2007, while massively rigged by the PDP as usual, provided an opening. As Umaru Yar'Adua took office, a tentative effort to reverse the scorched-earth tactics of his predecessor, President Olusegun Obasanjo, commenced. Obasanjo, in an attempt to rein in the armed militias, had established an army-led joint task force (JTF) and constituted it into a vir-tual army of occupation in the delta region. The emergence of MEND in early 2006 and its ability not only to confront JTF with significant firepower but also to portray itself successfully on the Internet as the savior of the delta poor was clear indication that Obasanjo's strategy had failed.

Following a series of meetings between representatives of the federal gov-ernment and Ijaw community and youth leaders, a road map to peace in the oil region was agreed upon by both parties on 24 August, 2007. An eighteen-member joint committee on the implementation of the road map was consti-tuted in September to, in the words of the terms of reference, "develop and put forward for the consideration of the Federal Government other initiatives that may facilitate the rapid development of the Niger Delta and the establishment of good governance in the region" (Federal Government of Nigeria 2007). A key demand of the Ijaw leaders, supported by the recommendations of a fact-finding panel on the restive region established by President Obasanjo in his first term as president, was that a substantial percentage of the oil receipts, greater than the 13 percent stipulated by the 1999 constitution, should go to the oil-producing states. Obasanjo had ignored the report. In the course of his negotiations with the Ijaw leaders, President Yar'Adua was also reluctant to implement the recom-mendations. In the ensuing impasse, Godwin Abbe, a retired general and one of Yar'Adua's ministers, was given the task of enforcing peace in the region. The

JTF, temporarily put on a leash, was given the green light to accelerate its puni-
tive activities in the delta. MEND and other unaffiliated groups also returned to
the fray. Attacks on oil facilities, shootouts between MEND and JTF contingents,
and kidnappings of oil workers became the norm.

Matters came to a head in May 2009 when soldiers guarding oil equipment
belonging to Chevron, the oil company, came under attack by the warlords near
the city of Warri in the western delta. President Yar'Adua ordered full-scale
military operations. As helicopter gunships pounded the warlords' camps in the
creek villages, the former explained the situation to an anxious nation thus:

> Developments in the Niger Delta over the past few weeks
> have necessitated the decisive action against armed criminal
> elements who have hijacked genuine agitations in the region
> and constituted themselves into very real threat to Nigeria's
> national security and economic survival. (Yar'Adua 2009)

Several Ijaw villages, including Oporoza, Okerenkoko, Kunukunuma, and
Benikrukru, were flattened. Although there are no independent sources to con-
firm the scale of casualties, E.K. Clerk, an Ijaw leader, stated at the height of the
military attacks that "on the last count, over hundred innocent souls, women
and children have been destroyed and property worth millions of Naira totally
destroyed" (Bello 2011, 17).

On June 25, 2009, after JTF contingents had ransacked a large swathe of
the western delta, President Yar'Adua unilaterally declared an "amnesty and
unconditional pardon to all persons who have directly or indirectly participated
in the commission of offences associated with militant activities in the Niger
Delta" (Bello 2011, 19) Those militants who put down their guns, the government stated, would be enrolled in an amnesty programme that would train them
in new skills and reintegrate them into society. The bulk of the militants, clearly
outgunned, accepted. Unconfirmed reports of cash and promises of lucrative
government contracts sweetened the deal for the top commanders. A few die-
hards, still holding on to the MEND umbrella, vowed to fight on, pointing out
that the proposed amnesty was a palliative that ignored the main demands of the

delta people. MEND's last hurrah was the independence-anniversary bombing. It still mounts sporadic attacks on oil installations in the delta, but the fiery creature of 2006 through 2008 has clearly lost its teeth.

Save Nigeria Group (SNG)

As already stated, SNG is a child of circumstance. The coalition of powerful authoritarian forces in the PDP that came together to rig the 2007 general elections and return the party to power with Umaru Yar'Adua, the ailing former governor of one of the northern states, as president had their project plunged into profound crisis when Yar'Adua fell ill yet again in November 2009. Conveniently no arrangement was made to transfer executive power formally to Dr. Goodluck Jonathan, the vice president, as stipulated in the constitution, before the president was flown out of the country for medical treatment. Indeed a cold war of sorts had developed between Jonathan and the power cabal around President Yar'Adua, drawn mainly from the northern part of the country right from May 2007, when both were sworn in. The choice of Jonathan, a Christian Southerner from the Ijaw ethnic group in the delta, as vice president was dictated by cynical political considerations, a sop designed to placate the warlords who, by early 2007, had shut in a significant chunk of oil production. He was treated as an outsider by the president's men who, anxiously looking over their shoulders as their principal's health worsened, determined the North would have its full share of eight years in office as President Obasanjo, a Christian Southerner, had done, increasingly developed a siege mentality.

As days became weeks and it became clear the ailing president would be away for a long time, ordinary citizens began to demand that Jonathan take his place temporarily as the constitution spelled out. The power cabal had expanded in the president's absence, drawing in key members of the national assembly, the state governors, powerful army officers, and some influential businessmen. It was clear to the discerning that they were plotting the civilian equivalent of a military palace coup. Repeated attempts to browbeat the vice president into quitting failed. When the cabal defiantly ignored public demands that the true state of President Yar'Adua's health be made public, human-rights lawyers headed for the courts to seek a legal interpretation of the relevant section of the constitution in the event of the absence of a sitting president. Several independent newspapers, labour organizations, and pro-democracy activists also joined the fray, demanding that Jonathan be empowered immediately to assume the presidency.

SNG emerged in January 2010 as a loose amalgam of these forces intent on ending the political impasse in favour of the vice president. Indeed the latter, by displaying uncommon calm even as the storm raged, emerged in this period as a national hero of sorts—the life-saving rope the poorer sections of an increasingly desperate and bedraggled citizenry latched on to. On February 9, 2010, the cabal suddenly caved in, and Dr. Jonathan was quickly sworn in as acting president. While SNG and other pressure groups played important roles in bringing about this outcome, a senior government official also acknowledged that the US government had been pivotal in stabilizing the country in that turbulent period and ensuring that Jonathan assumed power, in keeping with the intent of the constitution (*The Guardian* 2010).

SNG, according to its website, is a "nonprofit political society organization committed to creating a political environment that guarantees only the best, brightest, fittest and most competent Nigerians are democratically elected into public office." The group's "core beliefs and thrusts" are "unblocking and enlightening the minds of Nigerians with the message of political participation... [and] restoring sovereignty to Nigerians." Its adopted method of securing these objectives is "galvanizing a critical mass of men and women, boys and girls, old and young in the days and weeks ahead to challenge and change the status quo and say ENOUGH IS ENOUGH as we join hands to demand a Nigeria that befits Nigerians" (Save Nigeria Group 2012). SNG's national convener is Tunde Bakare, a Lagos-based Pentecostal pastor. Unlike CD in its heyday with branches all over the country, SNG is primarily a Lagos-based organization. Again, while CD openly relied on financial contributions from affiliate organizations to fund its campaigns, SNG has not published the source of its funds. Media reports linking the group to certain wealthy politicians intent on using it to further their private political projects have been denied.

The death of President Yar'Adua in May 2010 and the subsequent confirmation of Dr. Jonathan as substantive president led SNG to change the main thrust of its campaign. General elections were due in April 2011, and the group declared it was determined to put to an end the usual practices of vote fiddling and violence that had marred previous polls, particularly in 2007. Said SNG convener Tunde Bakare in a major speech in Abuja on May 31, 2010: "I believe very strongly that if, as a country, we are able to get our electoral system right, then our challenges are half-solved. A credible election will lead to a credible government" (Bakare 2010). A few months later, Bakare openly declared support for the Congress for Progressive Change (CPC), a new political party Muhammadu Buhari, a former military head of state, had established to enable him contest the presidency for the third time. Bakare was subsequently made his running mate. It is not clear whether Bakare consulted with and received the consent of other members of the SNG before he made the transition from the leader of a political-pressure group to a partisan politician. Indeed the national coordinator of the group later put out a press statement claiming "Pastor Bakare was suspended as a member of SNG in June 2010 when he tried to railroad the organization into partisan politics without the consent of its founding members and has not been readmitted since then" (*The Sun* 2012).

The period leading up to the elections was marked by bitter acrimony and a dangerous North-South divide as leading Northern members of the governing PDP dug in and insisted Jonathan rule himself out of the contest to enable a Northerner to fly the party flag and complete the late Yar'Adua's two terms, in keeping with an unwritten agreement that the presidency rotate evenly between North and South. Jonathan went ahead and contested and was declared the winner by the Independent National Electoral Commission, beating Buhari. Bakare declared the election a charade, returned to his church in Lagos, and sought to breathe new life into SNG.

Bakare and SNG's second moment in the sun came in January 2012 as President Jonathan, pointing to mounting fiscal problems, attempted to remove government subsidies on imported petrol. As petrol prices went up even in the midst of widespread economic difficulties, the outraged citizenry went on the warpath. Public demonstrations broke out spontaneously in several large cities. The Nigerian Labour Congress (NLC) and Trade Union Congress (TUC), the umbrella trade union organizations, declared a nationwide strike to force the government to retain the subsidy. SNG, with Bakare in the lead and in alliance with several pressure groups and human-rights organizations including the Joint Action Front, CD, and Enough Is Enough, called out the citizens of Lagos in a massive show of people power. After one week of fiery rhetoric and brinksmanship on both sides, government and labour officials stitched together an agreement partially removing the petrol subsidy. NLC called off the strike, and the public demonstrations instantly petered out even as Bakare continued to protest that the agreement did not receive the blessing of civil-society groups in the country (*The Nation* 2012).

The Jonathan government, exploiting Bakare's link to Buhari and the CPC, had, in the heat of the petrol-subsidy protests, portrayed Bakare and SNG in the media as the spearhead of a secret plot to bring about regime change in the country through undemocratic means. While Bakare robustly denied this damaging charge, his status as a card-carrying member of the CPC has significantly diminished the SNG in the public eye, enabling other umbrella pressure groups in the Lagos area espousing nonpartisanship to challenge his leadership role increasingly. Indeed the ease with which the government successfully out-manoeuvred SNG in a pivotal moment in the nation's political history, just as it had done to CD in 1994 and MEND in 2009, points to a sombre portrait of early twenty-first-century social movements in Nigeria, walking the relentless circle of sudden efflorescence followed soon after by decline, intrepid walkers lost in the political wood and unable to find the direction home. Why is this so?

Failing While Still Standing Tall

From 1900 onward Nigeria, the colonial state, not only deployed power in aid of its economic project of profitably exploiting the natural resources of the local people; it also sought to manage this power in such a way as to make resistance to it difficult. Even as the central state was being bolstered and given control of strategic resources, its local variants, in the form of warrant chiefs and "native" courts that colonial officials claimed upheld "native" law and customs, ensured that civic and economic life rotated on a narrow social axis, defining colonial subjects variously as "sons of the soil" and "strangers." Previously these categories had not existed; where they had, they were malleable and open to negotiation. Required to sell their produce at unfavourable prices to colonial authorities and sat upon by local despots propped up by the state, local people were reduced to poverty and powerlessness as the state further elaborated its power project in the 1930s and 1940s.

The colonial state was not a developmental state, nor did it speak the language of democracy. Whether residents in the emerging cities or the rural villages, the colonial subjects knew only deprivation and the usurpation of their political rights. Welfare associations, relying on kin in these harsh cities, were subjects' attempts to find the succour denied them by the state. Thus was civic virtue transformed into ethnic virtue, and the subjects found themselves active collaborators in the state's project of forging so many distinct competing ethnic groups. The subsequent politicization of these social identities as ethnic and political entrepreneurs went out in search of votes in the evening of colonial rule in the 1950s, and their consolidation into tribal mobs at each other's throats as the postcolonial state failed to deliver democracy and prosperity from the early 1960s onward is a tragic story told across the continent in this period.

For social movements in Nigeria and elsewhere in Africa, then, the fundamental challenge is how to engage fruitfully the original colonial burden of unaccountable power and poverty, currently replicated across the continent by indigenous successors. The post-World War II civic flowering that Adebayo Olukoshi drew our attention to (see above) offers a clue as to how this task might be achieved. The Zikist movement was established in 1947 by intrepid young men determined to end colonial rule, drawing inspiration from the writings of Dr, Nnamdi Azikiwe, the leading nationalist politician of that period following the death of his mentor, Herbert Macaulay (Okoye 1979). The Zikists not only understood the raison d'être of colonial power; they understood too that it deliberately dispersed itself into so many authoritarian and tax-farming ethnic enclaves in the local state to impoverish, divide, and ultimately pulverize resistance. The Zikists' answer to this complex challenge was to state unequivocally that the colonial condition was the fundamental cause of the subject's poverty; that it wanted to take power from the colonial state in order to deploy it for the economic benefit of local people; and that the way to go about this was to birth a movement transcending the freshly minted ethnic barriers in a double movement challenging the central colonial state and its many local variants.

Although the colonial state subsequently crushed the Zikists, their reading of the political terrain and the pan-ethnic strategy they devised to speak to it provide a useful lens through which to view the three social movements under consideration. CD, while able to establish branches across the country, saw itself primarily as a pro-democracy movement, a catalyst for change, while leaving the real game of political power to politicians. While African social movements need not make the taking of political power a sole and explicit goal, it is poor strategy to assume that even the modest civic demands they elect to make will be implemented by angel politicians descending from heaven. Indeed, given the extraordinary ability of incumbent power not only to set the rules of the political game but also to determine who gets to play it in a continent that is still fitfully making the transition to democratic consolidation, it is foolhardy not at least to take interest in potential political players and how those who best represent what the social movements are demanding might be made allies. CD's three mistakes—a faction of its supporting General Abacha's self-serving project in 1993, declining to challenge NADECO's regionalist strategy in 1994, and refusing to transform into a political party or actively support one in 1998—all proceeded from a limited understanding of the nature of incumbent power in 1990s Nigeria and how it might have been displaced.

MEND is primarily a local movement focused on the delta region and the travails of its inhabitants. While the movement echoed the civic and liberating language of local NGOs, it failed to adopt their pan-Niger Delta, national, and international outlooks and recruit their traditional allies in the media and the human-rights and pro democracy communities. Worse, MEND believed it could outgun a state that has, since colonial times, taken on and vanquished all challengers on the battlefield. Adopting a counterstrategy, the Nigerian government was able to reduce the MEND challenge to an ethnic Ijaw problem and sought out tribal mediators to resolve it. Left in the lurch were millions of impoverished local inhabitants of Ijawland and other parts of the region whose core grievances these mediators and the government alike ignored. Further, since the movement had no interlocutors in the human-rights and pro-democracy communities, the government was able to exploit MEND's tactic of kidnapping oil workers for ransom and reduce its project to banditry. The subsequent military action and the amnesty programme were really the last skirmishes in a war that had already been won by the state on both intellectual and political terrains.

Like the Zikist movement before it, the Save Nigeria Group makes it explicit that it is a political-pressure group, and its mission is to bring about a political order in which only the best and brightest get to serve the country. In a post-Soviet world, the only acceptable way of taking power is through democratic means, through the vehicle of the political party. Political parties are in turn defined by their policies and programmes. While Tunde Bakare and some of his key lieutenants are members of the Congress for Progressive Change, it is not at all clear that they have been successful in carrying along the majority of the members of the group.

Indeed SNG is like CD—a loose federation of several organizations that espouse diverse concerns and come together only to mount campaigns when there is sufficient consensus. Even if we were to concede that CPC is their joint political vehicle, the party has not yet offered a clear analysis of the country's social and economic problems and what definite policies and programmes it has devised to tackle them in a rapidly globalizing world. Further, the ease with which NLC and the federal government outmaneuvered SNG and reached a private understanding on the fuel subsidy drama in January 2012, even as SNG was in absolute control of people's power in the country's most populous city, raises questions about this movement's understanding of the nature of power in present-day Nigeria and its ability to forge alliances with other critical counter-vailing power centres across the country.

Even so, the speed and ferocity with which ordinary people responded to the central government's petrol-subsidy removal across the country in January 2012, and the ease with which Lagos slipped back into its traditional role as Nigeria's primary civic bastion during the protests, suggests the forces peace-fully pressing for a new political order founded on equity and shared prosperity, while still largely comatose and badly organized, have not collapsed altogether. The challenge is to relight the torch and use its light to chart a new path toward renaissance.

Conclusion

TY Bello, a budding Nigerian singer, states in the album sleeve of her hit single "The Future":

> In my view the [Abuja] bombings are a metaphor of the hopelessness and impending tragedy that may lie ahead if we do not become more engaged in building the country we desire. I realize that the crisis in the nation is beyond the political. We need to personalize Project Nigeria and take a stand for Nigeria NOW." (Bello 2010)

These words capture the frustrations, hopes, and promise of a new generation of Africans rapidly coming of age in a globalized world even as the continent continues to be racked by unaccountable rule, deepening poverty, and resurgent ethno-nationalism. It is precisely these challenges that the three social movements under study emerged to tackle, each in its own way. These three ailments, not surprisingly, replicate the colonial condition, leading us to conclude that the nature, objectives, and strategies of power in colonial Nigeria still persists in its postcolonial aftermath. The inability of Nigerian social movements, the three in particular, to come to terms with this sobering reality and tailor their strategies accordingly accounts for their modest gains in the field of struggle.

Neoliberal economic policies imposed on Nigeria and other African states from the early 1980s onward have proven to be disastrous failures even as economic managers peddling dubious statistics continue to assure bedraggled citizens that prosperity is imminent. The political double of these economic policies, liberal democracy, has recorded modest gains, but even countries that have entered the hallowed hall of democratic consolidation are still fragile, buffeted by a global economic order that makes it difficult for them to grow the prosperous citizenry and accompanying civic virtues that are the indispensable props of democracy properly understood. Civil society, hemmed in by poverty and unaccountable rule and divided by ethnic hegemons unleashed by incumbent power since colonial times, is unable to regenerate Jürgen Harbemas's famed "public sphere" as a prelude to democratising this power.

The portents are indeed dire, further complicated by the haemorrhaging of brainpower on the continent even as the neoliberal moment continues to prosper. What the deepening crisis requires, then, is an intellectual response linked to a robust civic programme that should count among its objectives forging an alliance with political actors pursuing the goals the three social movements we have studied set out to secure. It will not be an easy task to make the civic completely distinct from the explicitly party-political, as the primary vehicle with which to engage an authoritarian and self-serving state. However, progressive think tanks allied with academics, and pan-national NGOs forging productive relationships with the former even as they serve as a catalyst for trade unions, professional associations, women, and youth groups and other civic associations, can expand the field of political engagement, define and shape the agenda of public-policy discourse, and, with citizen-led democracy secured, serve as its ultimate protector.

Bello sings a stirring and beguiling song even as she declines to engage explicitly the political. Still, the beauty of her music and its powerful lyrics ultimately give hope to those intrepid others labouring to bring about the provident and self-restraining political kingdom.

References

Bello, O. 2011. *FG Orders JTF Ceasefire: FNDIC Role.* Warri, Nigeria: Delta Vanguard.

Bello TY, *The Future*, 2010, Chocolate City Records, A 6108763

Bakare, T. 2010. "2011: Campaign for Free, Fair and Credible Polls." Address presented at the International Conference Centre, Abuja, May 31, 2010.

Burkhalter, H. 1993. "Human Rights and Political Developments in Nigeria." Testimony before the House Foreign Affairs Committee on African Affairs, Washington, DC, August 4, 1993.

Dare, S. 2007. *Guerrilla Journalism: Dispatches from the Underground.* Ibadan: Kraft Books.

Falola, T. and J. Ihonvbere. 1985. *The Rise and Fall of Nigeria's Second Republic, 1979-1984.* London: Zed Books.

Federal Government of Nigeria. 2007. "Terms of Reference of the Joint Committee on the Implementation of the Agreed Roadmap to Peace in the Ijaw Areas of the Niger Delta." Letter to Oboko Bello, September 17, 2007, Federal Ministry of Information, Abuja, Nigeria.

Forrest, T. 1995. *Politics and Economic Development in Nigeria.* Boulder, Co: Lynne Rienner.

Ijaw Youth Council. 1998. *The Kaiama Declaration.* Port Harcourt: Ijaw Youth Council.

Jega, A., ed. 2000. *Identity Transformation and Identity Politics Under Structural Adjustment in Nigeria.* Uppsala and Kano: Nordiska Afrikainstitutet in collaboration with the Centre for Research and Documentation.

Okonta, I. 2006. "Behind the Mask: Explaining the Emergence of the MEND Militia in Nigeria's Oil-Producing Niger Delta." Accessed April 2013. http://oldweb.geog.berkeley.edu/ProjectsResources/ND%20Website/NigerDelta/WP/11-Okonta.pdf.

Okoye, M. 1979. *A Letter to Dr Nnamdi Azikiwe. A Dissident remembered.* Enugu: Fourth Dimension.

Olukoshi, A. 1997. "Associational Life" in L. Diamond, A. Kirk-Greene, and O. Oyediran, eds. *Transition without End: Nigerian Politics and Civil Society Under Babangida.* Boulder: Lynne Rienner.

Save Nigeria Group. 2012. "About Save Nigeria Group (SNG)." Accessed June 13, 2012. http://savenigeriagroup.com/about.php.

Mendelsohn, Daniel. 2010. "But Enough about Me." *New Yorker*, January 25.

Newspapers

1. *African Guardian*, October 16 1989 ("Dawn of a New Socio-political Order", an address to the nation by General Ibrahim Babangida).

2. *Thisday*, June 3 2012 ("MKO and the Last Flight to Johannesburg").

3. *The Nation*, June 5 2009 ("Why Military Action is On in the Niger Delta", by President Yar'Adua).

4. *The Guardian*, August 8 2010 ("What US' Hillary Clinton and Nigeria's Ajumogobia Discussed")

5. *The Sun*, January 20 2012 ("Save Nigeria Group Disowns Bakare").

6. *The Nation*, January 18 2012 ("Save Nigeria Group Threatens Court Action").

7. *The Sun*, March 25 2012 ("Olisa Agbakoba: I have power to predict the future").

CHAPTER 6

CLIMATE-JUSTICE-DRIVEN SOCIAL MOVEMENTS: ALTERNATIVE DEVELOPMENT FORCES OR AGENTS OF CHANGE IN AFRICA

Fidelis Allen

Africa is currently in an era in which many civil-society groups in the world, especially from developing countries, are demanding alternative development models. The neoliberal order under which politics and economy are organised seem clearly to have failed to tackle basic issues of development in the continent. Many activists are therefore asking for change.

There is increasing worry about the problems of industrial pollution, rising unemployment, poverty, climate change, political manipulation, human-rights abuses, poor public-service delivery, and so on. In South Durban, for example, residents of communities where South Africa's major oil refineries and other manufacturing companies are situated are well known for regular and fearless opposition to industrial pollution (Weston 2011; Pithouse

2006).[1] They are able to link environmental issues (such as climate change, oil spills, and so on) with general welfare issues (such as poor public-service delivery, unemployment, electricity poverty, inequality, and health) and wider social, political, and economic changes in the country. Durban as a whole can even be regarded as a centre of civil-society activism over domestic and global environmental issues that are easily linked to other areas of the development of South Africa.

After two decades of feet dragging and denial by many, a critical mass of diverse extractions of the global environment movement as well as business and political elites has come to acknowledge the reality and science of climate change. The crisis is rooted in the abuse of fossil fuel by more-affluent nations (Bassey 2011, ix). The ecological cost has echoed time and again. African countries contribute a marginal 3.5 percent of the total greenhouse gases in the atmosphere responsible for climate change; developed countries carry most of the blame for contributing the greatest amounts of greenhouse gases into the atmosphere through their years of industrialisation and their romance with fossil fuel. They are now said to be indebted ecologically to the world and its inhabitants.

As far as the field of political ecology in Africa is concerned, the extractive industry is at the heart of the looming climate catastrophe. Destructive production and distribution in the sector is pronounced all over Africa. There is no need to repeat what the science of climate change is saying. The colonial and neocolonial roots of the plundering of the continent without consideration for the climate or environment are an important part of the crisis story. As the science of climate change continues to give resounding warnings of danger and an impression that we do not have much time to stay aloof, the questions of a safer mode of development and energy production are at stake. In the meantime African political elites seem detached from the real answers to this crisis. On a general note, most people in the continent are pessimis-

---

1 Members of South Durban's Community Environmental Alliance (SDCEA), who are mainly residents of the southern areas of the city, regularly face issues ranging from industrial pollution to poor municipal government-service delivery. I have visited these mainly Indian and black communities extensively. Oil-refining activities in the area have created pollution-related health issues for which, for instance, the SDCEA has been fighting. Kennedy Road became famous for the housing crisis between the government and a shack-dwellers' movement.

tic about the African political elite when it comes to assessing their roles in developing Africa.[2]

Since independence, many African countries have seen increasing poverty, inequality, and unemployment. With an impression of inability or a failure to address these problems, some scholars have described African political elites as suffering from political paralysis. This in itself is seen as part of the overall development problems of Africa. According to Patrick Bond (2012), "elite paralysis is a crucial element in the politics of climate injustice."

Political elites have shown die-hard preference for neoliberal strategies of tackling climate change whereas pressure by justice-based groups to renounce neoliberal strategies is mounting on the United Nations and the governments of African states. These groups are pushing for the option of energy production and a consumption system in which fossil fuel can play an insignificant role. But the African political elite cannot easily follow their suggestions. Mainly they are systemically regulated to favour neoliberal solutions to societal problems. With the ecological issue increasingly taking a prominent position on the political agenda of development in Africa, the question of how to overcome these excesses has become critical.

In the context of dialectical[3] analyses of connections[4] between ecological economics, political ecology, and social movements in Africa, political ecologists have accused Marx (1885) of being guilty of neglecting environmental issues, or nature, in his analysis of the reproduction of capitalism. He discussed the circular flow of capitalist production and crisis without the component of envi-

---

2   Femi Anikulapo Kuti clearly represented this class of Africans with his response in an interview with a journalist recently, on his fiftieth birthday: "I think it is a big deal for us because most of us die young here in Nigeria. If you survive till fifty, it is a big deal because of the stress in our country—no electricity, health care is zero, one can't feed one's family, nothing works in this country. It is so stressful" (Kuti 2012)

3   Although there are various strands of dialectics today, *dialectics* refers to the science of motion, contradiction, and opposition that relays the idea of inevitability of change. As a way of looking at the world, dialectics is intended in Marxist theory to guide worker movements in their struggles for a just and equitable society. According to Rob Sewell, it is similar to a compass or map, which allows us to get our bearings in turmoil and permit us to understand the underlying processes that shape our world (Sewell 2002). Classical Marxist theory of economic crisis follows this thinking, in which the inevitability of the crisis of capitalism will lead to higher and more-qualitative forms of polity. The process is defined by the logic of dialectical materialism, on which the whole idea of contradiction or opposition (negation of the negation) is predicated. See S.G. McNall (1979).

4   One aspect of the logic of dialectics is the certainty of change. But what role should social movements play in this process? They are agents of change with respect to direct and indirect involvement with the change process.

ronmental crisis. Instead he saw nature as a free gift. This has been critiqued by political ecologists.[5] The good news is we can draw links between Marxism, political ecology, ecological economics, and movement building. As some social-movement scholars have argued, in the absence of revolutionary worker movements in the twenty-first century, environmental movements can play significant roles in orchestrating radical change in society (Clark and Foster 2010).

Against this backdrop this paper examines the prospects of climate-justice-driven radical social movements for the pursuit of broader political, economic, and environmental objectives in Africa. The paper relies on data-library materials and documents, interviews with activists in Durban and Niger Delta, and the author's personal observations of the activities of activists. We assume that ecological issues can play important roles in the rise of local social movements and their intolerance for market solutions to climate change, poverty, hunger, unemployment, inequality, elite manipulation of political processes, and destruction of ecosystems. These developments hold out many tendencies including the platform for designing alternative models of development in which the downtrodden classes will be at the centre of politics and the organization of production.

Political Elites and the Task of Development in Africa

Mounting cynicism about the capacity and willingness of the African political elite to pursue development[6] objectives that deliver quality living standards to ordinary citizens in the continent is not unconnected to the disappointments from the years of the postcolonial neoliberal state. Policy response by elites to critical issues such as poverty, inequality, unemployment, climate change, and so on seems to have created only more problems. Elites are accused of anti-people policies, practices, and positions that work against the development expectations of the citizens. Based on the assessment of state-society relations in recent times, a majority of Africa's political elites hardly see the welfare of their citizens

---

5   For an alternative vision of Marxian thinking in its relation to ecology, see Foster (2009; 2000) and Burkett (1999).

6   The culture of defining development in terms of growth, gross domestic product, or per capita income of a country does not address how the income is distributed. It does not account for rising poverty and unemployment amid rising statistics of growth as is currently the case in Nigeria. Even the Human Development Index approach of the United Nations Development Programme, which captures economic and non-economic factors, is flawed due to the influences of Western standards in the measurement of development. The concept is value laden. See Rist (2009).

as a priority. The net result is the downward trend the continent has taken (Bond 2006). According to Moeletsi Mbeki, "the political elites that took over African countries in the 1960s...saw government as a source of power and personal enrichment" (Mbeki 2005). He describes them as predatory and argues that "at the root of Africa's problems are the ruling political elites that have squandered the continent's wealth and choked its productivity over the last 40 years."

This explanation seems truer every day. African leaders seem to have used state power mostly as a mechanism to line their pockets with public funds. Many examples exist including Nigeria, where some politicians and business elites have perpetrated a dozen decades of imposition of pain on ordinary citizens through corrupt and agonising oil production, fuel marketing, and subsidy regimes. An ongoing government probe into the oil industry points to massive corruption in the oil establishment. Oil companies seem to have upheld their licenses to operate with corruption and political influence (Nwokoji 2012; Udo 2012). Recall multinational corporations paying vast amounts of money into the account of President Obiang Nguema of Equatorial Guinea (Mbeki 2005). This evil and corrupt collusion between many African leaders and multinational corporations has reached critical mass and has worked against the interest of development in Africa. If corruption blocks development (Ologbenla 2007), its origins are colonial, as stressed by William Gumede (2010): "In most African colonies, the colonial elite centralised political power, economic and civic power.... The institutions that should traditionally serve as watchdogs against corruption...served only the elite."

After the years of colonial afflictions and plunder, a transformation process that delivers to citizens' political and economic freedom was crucial. The early postcolonial era ought to have defined the future of these countries and their citizens. The political class was either too carried away by the euphoria of political independence or unaware of the conspiracy and technology of the neocolonial project. Whatever the case they used and continue to use state power for the perpetuation of colonial-style oppressive plundering of Africa's resources.

Colonialism reconfigured the continent into extractive and monocultural economies to serve the interests of a postcolonialist exploitative regime. The political class that emerged just before or shortly after independence could not suspect the veil but jumped at the opportunities of becoming the new lords.

They followed one process after another in response to the vagaries of modernity. "The way states and development specialists rationalise how to commit economic resources to development is influenced, to a greater extent by their level of persuasion towards specific development theories on Africa's development," wrote Matunhu (2011, 65).

The problem is dominant theories prescribe a Western-style pattern of development in which anything different in politics, economy, culture, technology, or agriculture is not seen as fitting for progress. It explains underdevelopment and the way to deal with it, insisting on Western models as the solutions. External factors are isolated in the explanation of the development woes. Instead, internal factors that often lead to externally determined suggestions point to policies, programmes, and actions that clearly have Western interest overtones. Both the structural adjustment programmes of the late 1980s and 1990s and current carbon-trading mechanisms for mitigating climate change are grounded in the economic gains expected by neoliberal business and political elites.

The mistaken idea and pursuit of economic growth as development are embedded in the modernisation school.[7] Modernisation was offered as a development framework by Western scholars on the eve of the independence of many African countries as part of the project to secure a knowledge infrastructure that supports or facilitates the reconfiguration of the continent into extractive economies. According to Richard Peet and Elaine Hartwick (2009,104), "modernisation theory, sociology's influential account, of development, is excessively Eurocentric in terms of its account of the universal supremacy of Western rationalism and Western institutions. Modernisation theory basically says: if you want to develop, be like us (West)". This idea of development took away political creativity, leaving political elites as mere actors of a script written by the West.

Modernisation reflects these values and serves as an instrument of advancement of the colonial project within a neocolonial Africa. As Stephen McCloskey (2009) argues, "Modernisation is a process whereby societies move from one condition to another, from a starting point to an end point." In Africa this tran-

---

7 Modernisation is a development thinking rooted in capitalism that started in the 1950s. It was not a coincidence that it emerged during a time when many African countries were seeing the last days or years of direct colonial control of their territories.

sition is ever guided by the principles of free-market systems. It involves free trade and access to key economic activities and resources of these countries by imperialist powers. Unfortunately the postcolonial politicians have continued to follow this mode of thinking about development, which has done nothing to change the living conditions of Africa's citizens.

Not even the global economic slump of 2008, which seems clearly incomplete as of today, has changed the role of political elites as accomplices in the survival and expansion of capitalism. Consequences of the policy makers' excesses are seen in the rising levels of hunger, homelessness, poverty, dictatorship, and corruption and the threat of extinction of human and nonhuman life due to rising global temperatures. These issues are shaping a specific kind of thinking about development and the role of a radical civil society. From the standpoint of critiquing the modernisation theory, capitalism, best represented by the activities of multinational corporations, plays a significant role in the political, economic, and environmental failures of Africa.

A section of the analyses of this development dilemma argues that since independence, political elites have concentrated on nation building in African countries in efforts to tackle the problems created by arbitrary sharing of Africa by Europeans in 1884 and 1885 (Sall 2004, 495). The nationalist political elites had feared the postcolonial state would be characterised by political struggles to overcome these arbitrary boundaries. On the contrary African international wars of boundary adjustments are rare. In fact, apart from Tanzania and Uganda, no countries in the continent have fought boundary redrawing wars. But internal wars proliferate. Wars of secession (as in Nigeria from 1967 to 1970, Sudan, and Senegal) reflect the nation-building gaps Europeans created. Political elites were distracted by nation-building projects and prevented from seeing the capitalist influence behind the scene.

Ecological Crisis

Political-ecological interactions have exploded over the last two decades. It shows in the numerous campaigns against the environmental consequences of human activities. Whether in the Niger Delta, where the oil industry has imposed severe damage on the environment, or in South Durban, where industrial pollution has been a long-time routine, fingers are pointed at the neoliberal order as being responsible for the destructive nature of production. Even the neoliberal capitalists admit to this reality. Neoliberal capitalism is a serious challenge to development in Africa and the survival of the globe. Climate change, the seemingly most visible expression of the political-ecological interaction at the multilateral and national fronts, and a prominent source of political and environmental policy, is linked to capitalism.

Climate scientists have used paleoclimate methods and satellites to study how climate is responding to human activities. The results show how the Earth will be disproportionately affected. James Hansen refers to the current global warming as "a planetary emergency" with potentials of global temperatures rising beyond four to five degrees Celsius. Hansen has warned that the unabated use of fossil fuel is at the base of this emergency, which is not unconnected to the perception that the Earth is a system in which everything is connected (Hansen 2008; Hansen and Sato 2012). The destruction of the Earth is therefore a destruction of self (Gore 2007).

Emissions from fossil-fuel production and consumption systemically connect to nature and humans in a destructive way.

> A key challenge at the beginning of the 21st century is to de-carbonize and de-materialize the global economy in time to avoid irreversible changes to the global and the local environment while generating enough social and economic development opportunities to reduce poverty and inequity. (Glemarec and de Oliveira 2012, 200)[8]

The aftereffect of polluting the climate with dangerous gases is therefore universal although in varying degrees. Africa is one region with a propensity for severe impacts. According to experts signs of a looming global ecological

---

8 Glemarec and de Oliveira (2012) argue "there are four main development paradigms that dominate current debate on how best to meet the key properties—social, economic and environment—of sustainable development, namely, (1) growth-focused development paradigm, (2) a pro-poor growth development paradigm, (3) a green-growth development paradigm and (4) a resilient-growth development.' Although seen as mutually exclusive, these compartments complement each other. However, they are inadequate for the challenge of sustainable development. "The new sustainable development paradigm will require a substantial transformation of the present economic development model analogous to what transition economies underwent during the industrial revolution."

catastrophe are showing all over the continent. Extreme weather events in West Africa are already affecting rural peasant agriculture. Farmers and pastoralists have reported how the climate is changing and how it is already affecting them (Magrath 2010).

Rain-fed agriculture, which African farmers mainly practice, is being affected by extreme rains and heat. In the case of coastal areas in the Niger Delta—more than eight hundred kilometres—agriculture is increasingly becoming futile for many peasant farmers because of annual extreme floods. Those who live on the shorelines are very vulnerable. A minor rise in sea level could submerge their houses and farms. Meanwhile poverty is compounding the problem. According to United Nations Programme on Environment, five major areas in which the environment is being threatened in Africa are climate, freshwater, oceans, seas, and biodiversity. It disclosed recently in its *Global Environment Outlook* that between 1980 and 2000, drought disasters in Africa rose by 38 percent. Ethiopia's arid and semi-arid region, where a lack of water for human consumption, livestock, and crop farming is becoming acute, is a good example. About 80 percent of the people there cannot access water (UNEP 2012). The Intergovernmental Panel on Climate Change argues human activities cause climate change (IPCC 2007). It "will threaten the basic elements of human life such as access to drinking water, food, health, the use of land—which has always been taken for granted—and the environment," remarked Satish Kumar (2009, 122).

The international policy establishment recognises these challenges[9] but fails to look beyond market-based instruments for solutions (Slunge and Loayza 2012). Market instruments are inadequate for the new sustainable development paradigm (Garcia-Guadilla 2005).[10] Some have emphasised mainstreaming "environmental concerns and opportunities in national and sectoral plans,

---

9 Environmental or ecological issues were not on the political agenda of multilateral institutions until 1972, at the first United Nations conference on the human environment held in Stockholm. It was not a meeting of governmental leaders alone; environmental scientists and civil-society organizations were also there. The decision to establish the United Nations Environment Programme was made in that meeting. American biologist Barry Commoner was not happy as he felt governmental leaders should have made decisions about developing industries that do not pollute the atmosphere and not decisions about monitoring pollution. See Black (2012).

10 The neoliberal trajectory to which African leaders are inclined refers to policymakers' pious devotion to free-market principles at the national and multilateral fronts in addressing ecological issues. Critics point to the severe economic, social, environmental, and political impacts on ordinary citizens in Africa and how this is a galvanizing reaction from civil society.

strategies and policies" (Nunan, Campbell, and Foster 2012, 262). Organisations and relevant government ministries and agencies are expected to integrate these opportunities vertically and horizontally. The new development paradigm requires substantial social, economic, and political transformation (Glemerec and de Oliveira 2012). The pursuit of development depends on what policymakers see as development.

At the twentieth Earth Summit (Rio+20) in June 2012 in Rio de Janerio, the Organisation for Economic Cooperation and Development (OECD) urged "developing countries to adopt green-growth strategies in order to foster sustainable development" (Onuorah, Muanya, and Onomo 2012). They said this will "reconcile environmental goals with economic growth and poverty reduction." But the model fails to speak to the threats to ecosystems (Resnick, Tarp, and Thurlow 2012, 215), and it does not address the problem from the roots (Bond 2000). [11] The separation of environmental concerns from development ought to have become old-fashioned, but it has remained part of the language of policy elites. No up-to-date example surpasses Brazilian Foreign Minister Antonio Patriota's. He was reported as saying "the summit just can't be about the environment. It has to be about development" (Prada and Chestney 2012). This depicts a continuing displacement of environmental issues in the development debate by political elites in developing countries.

On the Roles of Social Movements

Can political ecological issues dialectically play roles in resolving the development question in Africa?[12] By analysing the nature of the climate crisis and the responses of climate-justice groups, we are able to respond affirmatively although the process of achieving this is very complicated. In essence while recognising the limited role political elites can play or have played in Africa's journey toward development, the robust and developmental roles civil-society or social movements are expected to play can be located in the inspiration provided by climate-justice activists. We must learn from those whose engagement with climate-justice issues

---

11 Critics point to neoliberalism's inability to tackle ecological or environmental issues associated with economic green growth.

12 Patrick Bond (2012) discusses the frustration with climate policy elites in South Africa and multilateral arenas. In his new book, he explains the rise of climate justice as a movement from below.

implies a quest for a development alternative that speaks to the very foundation of the economic, political, environmental, and social well-being of citizens. Some social-movement scholars have predicted that in the absence of radical labour movements in the twenty-first century, environmental movements will play very significant roles in driving social change (Clark and Foster 2010).

Before discussing the response of the climate-justice movement, we need to acknowledge generally that beside the climate issue, civil society's potential for driving change is well noted. It has played a relevant role in political struggles in many African countries. In South Africa civil society constituted a significant part of the liberation movement in the struggle against apartheid. The eventual takeover (transition) of power by Nelson Mandela or the African National Congress (ANC) was instructive (Ballard 2005, 77). In the Benin Republic, civil society's political and social-justice struggles led to the national conference of 1989, in which important political decisions about democracy in the country were made. In Nigeria the student movement played a good role in the abrogation of a proposed Anglo-Nigerian pact in 1962. The students were active in the anti-SAP riots of the 1980s. Youth filled the ranks of groups that resisted Shell in Ogoniland and have been active in resisting further attempts by the company and the federal government to resume oil production in the area. Campaigns by Ogoni youth against the government's seeming lack of interest in the implementation of UNEP's environmental assessment report on Ogoniland, which implicated Shell in oil degradation of the land, soil, and air, are ongoing.

It took eighteen days of democratic protests by the youth to get President Mubarak of Egypt to step down on February 11, 2011 after thirty years of rule.[13] Similarly it took twenty-eight days to put an end to Tunisian President Ben Ali's twenty-three-year-old regime. This was how easily old-fashioned, undemocratic regimes (including the controversial case of Libya) were terminated or shaken by citizens. These are highly contentious issues whose outcomes can sometimes

---

13   The Egyptian uprising of January 25, 2011, which led to the removal of President Hosni Mubarak, has yet to achieve results that speak to issues of unemployment, hunger, dictatorship, and so on in the country. Instead neoliberal forces are at work to determine the political process and outcome. The military and political establishments are mainly out to reestablish the old order, in which the people who gathered at Tahrir Square can remain marginalized. The march toward democracy is a long road and guided by the military.

be difficult to conclude. But a few lessons are clear, including the role of social movements in political struggles. They stand in contrast to formal political-opposition groups, such as political parties, as pillars and hope for the common man on the street. Jean-Pierre Filiu identifies the lesson of anger and the power of younger generations against oppressive and authoritarian regimes. As he notes, "Young activists are proud to be at the vanguard of democratic protests, and the *shehab* [youth] paid a high price" (Filiu 2011, 31). Such prices can only be offered when the perceived value of or reward for inaction is less than what can be seen as gain from participating. The greatest lesson perhaps is the notion of political and economic change possibilities from a determined civil-society opposition in search of opportunities to "renegotiate citizens' rights" (Sall 2004).

Since the secession of South Sudan in 2011, Sudan is proving to have a student movement with the capacity to attract people of all walks of life in protests against economic difficulties imposed by neoliberal policies and manipulations by external forces. The government, which had depended mainly on oil revenues before the secession, will have to go without at least three-quarters of the revenues they had accrued from prior oil production. This means adjustments in national budgets and measures to fill the gaps. President Omar Hassan Ahmed al-Bashir's government recently announced budget cuts of \$2.4 billion, the removal of fuel subsidies, and increased taxes and custom duties on opulence commodities. Meanwhile oil production in South Sudan has been shut down because of disagreements with Sudan over benefits from oil. At issue is the role the neoliberal oil establishment played in these difficulties, the reactions of citizens, and threats of war between the countries after many years of wars of secession (Dorsey 2012).

Ecologically Driven, Radical Social-Movement Actors

Radical social movements are simply a collection or coalition of social-movement groups driven and persuaded by values that repel inequality, the destruction of ecosystems, poverty, hunger, unemployment, climate change, market solutions to environmental problems, corruption, and capitalism. They are also determined to stop or withdraw their political support from regimes' policies and seek solutions other than neoliberalism.

In Africa, South Durban and Nigeria's Niger Delta are leading centres of the activities of community-based environmental-justice groups. For example, the South Durban Community Environmental Alliance (SDCEA) provides leadership in tackling diverse issues including poor public-service delivery, unemployment, poverty, and industrial pollution. It uses methods of retail politics to engage the state and corporations on these issues on a regular basis. Climate issues are appreciated and resisted by many residents of the South Durban communities under its leadership thanks to the creative ways in which managers of the organisation have been able to link issues of climate change and general industrial pollution to poverty, unemployment, and the health of citizens. Likewise the Movement for the Survival of Ogoni People (MOSOP) and Nigeria's leading environmental organisation, Environmental Rights Action/Friends of the Earth (ERA/FoE), has campaigned against oil pollution and its after effects for decades. Climate issues are, however, not popular at the ethnic/grassroots level, which MOSOP represents.

"The prospect is there because environmentally conscious civil society actors in Africa are beginning to know that countries in the continent are being duped by capitalist greedy corporations," remarked Celestine Akpobari.[14] In a similar vein, Nigeria's foremost international environmental activist and chair of Friends of the Earth International, Nnimmo Bassey (2011), said, "Each new moment is a chance for a new movement. Each new minute another opportunity." The growing struggles of environmental groups over issues of livelihood, climate change (pollution), energy policy, inequality, conflict, and political and economic development at transnational and local fronts are capable of influencing the rise of national radical-social movements for bigger struggles.

Below are examples of how climate-justice activists' values, expectations, and demands can provide clues to this possibility. On the issue of climate change, as Bond and Erion (2009, 338) argue, radical and neoliberal approaches can be deployed to address the problem. The latter, which entails the status quo, is preferred by political elite. As earlier indicated, the former requires a valid transformation of the energy system, transport, and industry.[15] Values, expectations, and demands made by social

---

14 Telephone interview with Celestine Akpobari, June 22, 2012.

15 Ibid.

movements reflect either of these approaches as solutions to current ecological crises. Our argument, derived from activities of climate justice activists,[16] is that social movements in Africa can seize the opportunities ecological problems provide worldwide for broader social, economic, and political struggles and transformation.

Climate justice is a concept used to describe the new bottom-up movement that combines a number of issues in political ecology and ecological economics in the war on climate change. Its philosophy, ideology, principles, strategies, and tactics are predicated on a perceived need to fill gaps created by "the inability of global elite actors to solve major environmental, geographical, social and economic problems" (Bond and Dorsey 2010, 244).

It all started with an initial response by key environmental nongovernmental organisations in alliance with global political or climate-policy elites searching for solutions to climate change. It adopted an initial designation—the Climate Action Network (CAN)—in 1997. The movement emerged from this as a reaction to the failure of the collaboration within the United Nations Framework Convention on Climate Change (UNFCCC) to denounce emissions trading as a solution to climate change. It was more or less a movement away from how sections of the global civil society accepted the approach. Climate-justice activists see carbon trading as a false solution.[17] The movement's set of nonmarket proposals as an alternative is based on rational and objective critiques of carbon trading. Movement members have long withdrawn from multilateral climate-policy lobby sites to focus on direct actions against carbon trading. It draws inspiration from key fossil-fuel combustion sites around the world including Nigeria's oil-rich Niger Delta.

The transition from a lobby group within to a climate-justice movement spanned time and space.[18] Specific groups organised against different aspects of the global climate-policy establishment. Protests by groups against financial hegemony of the world by developed countries in the late 1990s, and the strug-

---

16 They believe environmental or climate-change issues are inherently connected to other issues such as unemployment, poor public health, inequality, poverty, hunger, and so on in which citizens worry about and expect governments to intervene. Fossil fuel is regarded as a major issue in this debate.

17 This refers to series of market-based solutions to climate change. The common thread is the focus on carbon trading including offset mechanisms, intergovernmental negotiations for piecemeal emissions reductions, and regional and national subcarbon trading schemes promoted or supported by the United Nations.

18 This narrative is taken from accounts given by Patrick Bond and Michael K. Dorsey and from my observations of activities and conversations with activists at the Peoples Space during COP 17 in November and December 2011.

gles for global justice in 1999 and the 2000s, typified by the Seattle protest against the World Trade Organisation, represent this transition. Furthermore there was the emergence of the Durban Climate Justice Group in 2004 and its critique of government and corporate environmental practices. The emergence of the Climate Justice Now! network in 2007 and the birth of the European Climate Justice Alliance in the wake of the Copenhagen Conference of Parties in 2009 are part of this transition and the shape the movement started to assume. Current radical critiques of multilateral climate-policy framework by the Malaysian Third World Network and its extensive mobilisation work in preparation for a maiden 2010 World People's Conference on Climate Change and Rights of Mother Earth in Cochabamba is worth noting.[19] The Detroit branch of the World Social Forum helped consolidate mobilisation and awareness through its activities in the United States of America the same way the European Climate Justice Alliance influenced populations through its major events and programmes on climate justice in different locations throughout Europe.

Besides revealing the formative stages, this transition account shows the maturity process, challenges, and the future of the movement. The groups' activities are not only interrelated; they speak to the global energy establishment, transport and industry, and the urgent need to transform the same from their current fossil-fuel-intensive economies. For example, on the eve of the United Nations Conference of Parties Number 17 in Durban last year, South Africa's respected nongovernmental organisation, groundWork, organised a workshop in Durban called The Dirty Energy Week.[20] Several nongovernmental groups from different parts of the world that attended denounced present energy production and consumption patterns in the world. "Leave the oil in the soil," remarked Bassey, who addressed the plenary. The message was clear about where the organisation and its members belong.

Already the movement has inspired several groups around the world. For example, community-based groups in the United States have organised several

19 Cochabamba is in Bolivia. It was a congregation of ecologists or climate-justice activists whose main concern was how to address the global threat of climate change from the perspective of global civil society.

20 It was held from November 22 to 25, 2011, three days before COP 17. It is significant in the sense that it brought together climate-justice activists who analysed various issues bordering on the relationships among environment, climate change, poverty, inequality, unemployment, political instability, and general development.

protest marches against coal power-plant projects. According to Patrick Bond and Michael Dorsey (2010), "Nearly two thirds of the 151 new power plant proposals from the Bush Energy Plan have been cancelled, abandoned or stalled since 2007—largely due to community-led opposition." These groups have further prevented the proliferation of incinerators and the expansion of big oil projects. In Richmond a coalition of groups blocked Chevron from expanding its refinery in court. Mega hydros have also suffered restrictions. The one in Klamath River was successfully resisted by local communities that forced Pacificorp Power Company to commit to removing it by 2020.

The need for a radical transition away from fossil-fuel production and consumption, which the movement privileges, led some scholars to propose eco-socialism (Kovel and Lowy 2001) as a viable alternative. Incidentally eco-socialist writings belong to the climate-justice literature. It is a strand in the attempt to combine ecological and Marxist thinking (Burkett 2006, 23). Some adherents have argued that this involves a transformation of needs and substantial leaning toward a quality of life that undercuts fossil fuel.

With fossil fuel having been an indispensable element of the capitalist order, scholars insist that undermining it in the new order will bring freedom to all confiscated lands and exploited people. This will lead to the defeat of a looming global ecological crisis. This view as well as its practicality, spread, and application depend much on other factors such as stronger labour input, the possibility of abundant green jobs, and a link between peace activism and climate justice. Wars and military-industrial establishments are fossil-fuel intensive and environmentally unfriendly. Finally, there is a need for increased presence and mobilisation of grassroots populations by environmentalists and eco-socialists in high-intensity fossil-fuel combustion sites.

There are numerous ideological orientations pulling the movement. This is evidenced in the rhetoric of climate justice within and outside the United Nations. A tendency to draw the movement into endorsing carbon trading remains high although, as Bond and Dorsey (2010) would argue, this rhetoric plays out at the level of political-elite processes. They use the language of the movement deceptively to sway members into analyses and actions that support neoliberal strategies. Ironically elites seem quite successful in their rhetoric of climate justice as evidenced in the current resistance of neoliberalism to major alternative proposals on climate change coming from the side of the movement.[21]

The rhetoric of climate justice and development has manifested within the ranks of the movement. The reason is in part the principle of *common but differentiated responsibility*, which some of the developed countries do not want to hear about today. In any case the movement seems much more strengthened at the moment. This was mostly achieved through the common demands in Cochabamba, which are as follows:

- A 50-percent reduction in greenhouse gas emissions by 2017.
- Stabilising temperature increase to 1°C and 300 parts per million (PPM) of carbon dioxide in the atmosphere.
- Acknowledging the climate debt owed by developed countries.
- Full respect for human rights and the inherent rights of indigenous people.
- A universal declaration of the rights of mother earth to ensure harmony with nature.
- Establishment of an international court of climate justice.
- Rejection of carbon markets and commodification of nature through the REDD programme (Reducing Emissions from Deforestation and Forest Degradation).
- Promotion of strategies that change the pattern of consumption in developed countries.
- Ending intellectual property rights for technology useful for mitigating climate change.
- Payment of 6 percent of developed countries' GDP to tackle climate change.

Each of these demands reveals a specific value, orientation, radicality, and ideological path as opposed to the neoliberal climate policy establishment. The movement's submissions to negotiators at the United Nations' Conference of Parties in Durban were also based on the above-stated demands but not without

---

21   The success of the 1996 Montreal Protocol, which banned chlorofluorocarbon as a measure for closing the hole in the ozone layer, was due to global political elites' willingness to address the problem. The same approach is needed in the case of climate change.

some moderate and liberal voices from the civil society. According to Samantha Hargreaves (2012), "Others from civil society had lower ambitions, seeking a 'fair ambitious and binding' deal that did include economic justice or trans-formation values." The South African host simply expected the maintenance of the Kyoto Protocol, particularly in the area of the common but differentiated responsibility principle. But this failed to materialise as hindrances manifested in the shifting of decisions about many issues to future meetings. This was in the interest of major developed countries like the US, as shown in the response of a State Department official, Trevor Houser, who remarked that the outcome was "promising because of what it did not say" (Hargreaves 2012). What he probably meant was that a climate-justice issue such as the principle of common but dif-ferentiated responsibility was repulsively inconsequential.

The conference eventually hooked carbon trading to the Kyoto Protocol, which many feared would collapse after 2012. For African women this means worsening social and economic conditions that will leave farmers unable to meet their food-security needs by 2100 (Hargreaves 2012). At least nine out of every ten farmers will not be able to produce food. About 180 million women will die as a result (Bond 2012). According to Nanganidzai Makoho[22] of the Rural Women Assembly and Climate Justice, "Climate change threatens women's live-lihood and their families." In a similar vein, Paulina Ledwaba argued, "I am here because the climate has changed, affecting my farming business."[23]

The United Nations Earth Summit (Rio+20) of June 2012 in Rio de Janerio was attended by 130 heads of states and more than fifty thousand people who were not governmental delegates, including climate-justice movement mem-bers from different regions of the world. The movement's demands were again based on the Cochabamba resolutions. But environmental groups seemed even more disappointed with the outcome as political and policy elites showed even more interest in economic growth than in the protection of the climate. Green-peace described the outcome of the summit as "pathetic" and argues, "Rio+20

---

22 Interviewed on December 4, 2012, in Durban.

23 Interviewed on December 3, 2012, in Durban. She was also among a team from Zimbabwe that participated in activities of civil society at the Peoples Space during COP 17 in Durban under the auspices of the Rural Women Assembly.

turned into an epic failure. It has failed on equity, failed on ecology and failed on the economy" (Margolis 2012). According to Meena Raman of the Malaysian radical Third World Network:

> The outcome document does not have the ambition needed to save the planet or the poor, but it has not taken us backwards. This minimal outcome signals a lack of political courage, leadership and commitment from developed countries and those campaigning for the future we really want, will have to redouble our efforts.

In a similar vein, Stephen Hale says, "We face connected crises. This should be a turning point, but it is a dead end" (Margolis 2012).

African political elites, along with their developed country counterparts, were accused of decisions that do not address the core issues of poverty, equity, and reductions in greenhouse gas emissions. Instead the rhetoric of climate justice resounded among the elites. One World Bank official reportedly spoke to developing countries of the need to go green and make growth responsive to global environmental safety. When this is put in the context of the many years of funding or promoting fossil-fuel energy projects in developing countries and their likely impacts on climate, one can wonder indefinitely about the sincerity of the comments. In any case the green-growth concept is seen by climate-justice groups as reformist and incapable of addressing their concerns, such as poverty and climate change.

Challenges

Despite prospects of an ecologically driven, radical social movement in pursuit of broader social, economic, environmental, and political goals, a range of issues challenge this outlook. For example, within the climate-justice movement there are contradictions between its radicalness and character as an oppositional force (Buttel and Taylor 1994, 244). The movement has yet to develop ways of dealing effectively with corporate vetoes of its proposals to problems of climate change. Likewise some movement groups have elected to work within the neoliberal framework and have aligned with global financial institutions like the

World Bank. These issues can hinder its potency to inspire national or local civil society effectively.

Ethnic and religious colours of civil-society groups in some parts of Africa will frustrate the unity and solidarity required to curtail the excesses of politicians. This is increasingly evident in the responses of civil-society groups to anti-people policies. For example, the leadership of Nigeria's Trade Union Congress and other civil-society groups were divided on ethnic and religious lines in the protest marches against the removal of fuel subsidy by the federal government in January 2012. Ethnic youth groups and ex-militants in the Niger Delta supported the decision, organised around it, and would later boast that the removal of the fuel subsidy exposed corruption in the oil industry. In contrast activists in the western and northern parts of Nigeria organised full-length resistance against the decision.

Unfortunately workers in many parts of Africa are consistently playing reactionary roles. In the case of the Nigeria National Petroleum Corporation (NNPC), management seems to bribe the leaders of the workers' union regularly.[24] Workers attend management courses designed to curtail their radicality and influence the content of their activism. Often this is at great cost to society. They have never taken issue with the environmental impact of oil companies' activities in their campaigns for improved living standards for its members. It is difficult to see workers in Africa with the revolutionary credentials for political and economic struggles.

The upheaval in Egypt is about unemployment, hunger, homelessness, police brutality, poverty, and neoliberalism. But the Egyptian labour union has played a insignificant role in these processes. "The nascent trade union movement in Egypt will need to develop political structures for the voices of the working class to be heard in electoral processes," remarked El-Hamalawy (2012) as he explained the problem of the lack of a working-class political platform in Egypt in the peoples' struggles against dictatorship and misrule. Labour could not even produce a candidate. According to Horace Campbell (2012):

---

24 Telephone interview with a senior staff of NNPC, June 22, 2012 (name withheld).

The Egyptian election results have shown that the state of the forces of repression must be dismantled before elections can have meaning. Experiences from Zimbabwe, Kenya and Uganda have pointed to the reality that progressives cannot hope to make real changes within electoral system that reinforces neoliberal economics and low intensity democracy.[25]

Conclusion

I have examined how global ecological issues can be deployed for broader social, economic, and political struggles against the excesses of the political elites in Africa including their pursuit of neoliberal policies. The net results, of which inequality and the destruction of ecosystems are the most prominent, might in the coming years be the basis of designing alternative models of development in which the downtrodden classes will be the central factor of politics and organisation of production. As well, they would be the basis on which any development model imposed by market-oriented political elites will be rejected and overturned through collective action. This implies movement into seasons of intolerance of corruption, rule of capital, inequality, poverty, climate capitalism, dictatorship, and exploitative economic and social systems. By inference climate-justice activists can serve as catalysts for change in Africa.

---

25 Horace Campbell argues that revolutions are not decided by elections. He seems to base his argument on the unfinished work of the civil society in Egypt.

References

Ballard, R. 2005 "Social movements in post-apartheid South Africa: An Introduction" in P. Jones and K. Stokke, eds. *Democratising Development. The Politics of Socio-economic Rights in South Africa*. Netherlands: Koninklijke Brill NV Leiden.

Bassey, N. 2011. *To Cook a Continent. Destructive Extraction and the Climate Crisis in Africa*. Oxford: Pambazuka Press.

Black, R. 2012. "Stockholm: Birth of the green generation." June 4. http://www.bbc.co.uk/news/science-environment-18315205.

Bond, P. 2012. *Politics of Climate Justice: Paralysis Above, Movement Below*. Pietermaritzburg: University of KwaZulu-Natal Press.

Bond, P. 2011. "Durban's Water Wars, Sewage Spills, Fish Kills and Blue Flag Beaches" in P. Bond, ed. *Durban's Climate Gamble. Trading Carbon, Betting the Earth*. South Africa: Unisa Press.

Bond, P. 2006. *Looting Africa: the economics of exploitation*. London: Zed Books.

Bond, P. 2000. *Elite Transition. From Apartheid to Neo-Liberalism in South Africa*. London: Pluto Press.

Bond, P. and Dorsey, M.K. "Anatomies of Environmental Knowledge and Resistance: Diverse Climate Justice Movement and Waning Eco-Neoliberalism." *Journal of Australian Political Economy* 66, December (2010): 286–316.

Bond, P. and Erion, G. 2009. "South African Carbon Trading: A Counterproductive Climate Change Strategy" in D.A. McDonald, ed. *Electric Capitalism: Recolonising Africa on the Power Grid*. Cape Town: HSRC Press.

Burkett, P. 2009. *Marx and Nature: A Red and Green Perspective*. New York: St. Martin's Press.

Burkett, P. "Two Stages of Ecosocialism? Implications of some Neglected Analyses of Ecological Conflict and Crisis." *International Journal of Political Economy*, 35, 3 (2006): 23–45.

Buttel, F. and Taylor, P. 1994. "Environmental Sociology and Global Environmental Change. A Critical Assessment" in M. Redclift and T. Benton, eds. *Social Theory and Global Environment*. London: Routledge.

Campbell, H. 2012. "Revolutions are not decided by elections. Lessons from the ongoing electoral processes in Egypt." Accessed December 2013. http://www.pambazuka.org/en/category/features/82593.

Clark, B. and Foster, J.B. 2010. "Marx's Ecology in the 21st Century." *World Review of Political Economy* 1, 1.

Kuti, Femi Anikulapo. 2012. "I thought I might die before 50." *Daily Independent*, June 16.

Dorsey, J.M. 2012. "Sudanese anti-government protests mushroom." Accessed April 2013. http://www.globalpolicy.org.

El-Hamalawy, H. 2012. "Egypt's working class and the question of organization." *Pambazuka*, Issue 587, Accessed December 2013, http://www.pambazuka.org/en/issue/587

Filiu, J.P. 2011. *The Arab Revolution. Ten Lessons from the Democratic Uprising.* Oxford University Press.

Foster, J.B. "Marx's Ecological Value Analysis." *Monthly Review* 52, 4 (2009).

Foster, J.B. 2000. *Marx's Ecology: Materialism and Nature.* Monthly Review Press.

Garcia-Guadilla, M.P. "Environmental Movements, Politics and Agenda 21 in Latin America." Civil Society and Social Movements Programme Paper no.16, United Nations Research Institute for Development, October 2005.

Glemarec, Y. and de Oliveira, J.A.P. "The Role of the Visible Hand of Public Institutions in Creating a Sustainable Future." *Public Administration and Development* 32, 3 (2012): 200–214.

Gore, A. 2007. *Earth in the Balance*. London: EarthScan Publications, Ltd.

Gumede, W. 2012. "Why fighting corruption in Africa fails." Accessed December 11, 2013 http://www.pambazuka.org/en/category/features/85443.

Hansen, J.E. 2008. "Tipping Point: Perspective of a Climatologist" in *Widlife Conservation Society, State of the Wild 2008–2009: A Global Portrait of Wildlife, Wildlands, and Oceans*. Washington, DC: Island Press.

Hansen, J.E. and Sato, M. 2012. "Paleoclimate implications for human-made climate change" in A. Berger, F. Mesinger, and D. Šijački, eds. *Climate Change: Inferences from Paleoclimate and Regional Aspects*. Springer.

Hargreaves, S. "COP 17 and Civil Society: The Centre did not Hold." Occasional Paper 64, Institute for Global Dialogue, May 2012.

Intergovernmental Panel on Climate Change. 2007. "Climate Change: Synthesis Report." Accessed April 2013. http://www.ipcc.ch/pdf/assessment-report/ar4/syr/ar4_syr.pdf.

Kovel, J. and Lowy, M. 2001. "An ecosocialist manifesto." Accessed April 2013. http://www.socialistvoice.ca/?p=146.

Kumar, S.M. 2009. "Climate Change and Development: Will growth End Poverty or the Planet?" in G. McCann and S. McCloskey, eds. *From the Local to the Global. Key Issues in Development Studies*. London: Pluto Press.

Magrath, J. "The injustice of climate change: voices from Africa." *Local Environment: The International Journal of Justice and Sustainability* 15, 9-10 (2010): 891–901.

Margolis, M. 2012. "Is Rio+20 Environmental Summit a Failure?." *The Daily Beast*, June 20.

Marx, K. 1885. *Capital. Volume II: The Process of Consultation of Capital.* Accessed April 2013. http://www.marxists.org/archive/marx/works/1885-c2/ch01.htm.

Matunhu, J. "A Critique of modernization and dependency theories in Africa: Critical assessment." *Africa Journal of History and Culture* 3, 5 (2011): 65–72.

Mbeki, M. 2005. "Liberate Africa from its Political Elites." *Wall Street Journal*, July 5.

McCloskey, S. 2009. "Introduction: Recasting Development in a Changing Global Economy" in G. McCann and S. McCloskey, eds. *From the Local to the Global. Key Issues in Development Studies.* New York: Pluto Press.

McNall, S.G. 1979. "Dialectical Social Science" in S.G. McNall, ed. *Theoretical Perspectives in Sociology.* New York: St. Martin's Press.

Nwokoji, C.T. 2012. "Multiple probes in oil sector threaten FDI inflow." *The Sun*, November 12.

Nunan, F., Campbell, A., and Foster, E. "Environmental Mainstreaming: The Organisational Challenges of Policy Integration." *Public Administration and Development* 32, 3 2012): 262–277.

Ologbenla, D.K. "Leadership, Governance and Corruption in Nigeria." *Journal of Sustainable Development in Africa* 9, 3 (2007): 97–118.

Onuorah, M., Muanya, C., and Onomo, A.A. 2012. "OECD lists benefits of 'green growth' for Nigeria, others." *The Guardian*, June 19.

Peet, R. and Hartwick, E. 2009. *Theories of Development: Contentions, Arguments, Alternatives.* New York: Guilford Press.

Pithouse, R. 2006. "Struggle is a School: The Rise of a Shack Dwellers' Movement in Durban, South Africa." *Monthly Review* 57, 9 (2006).

Prada, P. and Chestney, N. 2012. "Expectations low for Rio+20 UN development summit." Reuters, June 18.

Resnick, D., Tarp, F., and Thurlow, J. "The Political Economy of Green Growth: The Case from Southern Africa." *Public Administration and Development* 32, 3 (2012): 215–228.

Rist, G. 2009. *The History of Development. From Western origins to Global Faith.* London: Zed Books.

Sall, E. "Social Movements in the Renegotiation of the Bases for Citizenship in West Africa." *Current Sociology* 52, 4 (2004): 595–614.

Sewell, R. 2002. "What is Dialectical Materialism? A study guide with questions, extracts and suggested reading." Accessed April 2013. http://www.marxist.com/what-is-dialectical-matrialism.htm.

Slunge, D. and Loayza, F. "Greening Growth through Strategic Environmental Assessment of Sector Reforms." *Public Administration and Development* 32, 3 (2012): 245–261.

Udo, A. 2012. "Jonathan to receive Ribadu Panel, two other oil industry probe reports Friday." *Premium Times*, October 29.

United Nations Environment Programme. 2012. "Summary for Africa, The Eve of Rio+20." Acceessed December 13, http://www.unep.org/geo.

Weston, D. 2011. "The Politics of Climate Change in South Africa" in P. Bond, ed. *Durban's Climate Gamble. Trading Carbon, Betting the Earth.* South Africa: Unisa Press.

CHAPTER 7

PRIVATE MEDIA AND SOCIAL CHANGE IN AFRICA: ACHIEVEMENTS, LIMITATIONS, AND PROSPECTS

Mor Faye

For many centuries, to paraphrase Ivorian sociologist Francis Akindes (1995), slavery and colonization were the two major challenges faced successively by African societies. These challenges had the particularity of being external, and, although they have been more or less met, they have left deep scars and came back in other forms. Since independence in the 1960s, the main challenge African societies have faced has been an internal one: the democratic challenge. African states need to establish democracy and the rule of law in compliance with specific methods, and economic and social welfare must be achieved for all not just for the elite. Because these aspirations remain unfulfilled, due to the inertia of our political systems being faced with the requirements of democratization and the mismanagement of public funds, African societies experience cyclical and sometimes very violent social movements expressed through alternative channels of expression: the private media. Benin, Senegal, and Togo, which have been taken here as examples, have witnessed the rise of this type of media in recent decades (Faye 2008; Frère 2001). The private media define themselves as independent as opposed to the state media, which remain under the ideological, administrative, and editorial control of the governments in power.

The private media can be divided into three categories that have developed successively as the countries concerned began to experience a revival of political and media pluralism due to pressures exerted on the elite in power by the people and donors (Conac 1993) in the 1980s and 1990s, following a long period of political authoritarianism marked by civilian or military single-party systems. Chronologically speaking the first type of private media to emerge was private print media in the mid-1980s in Senegal and at the turn of the 1990s in Benin and Togo (PANOS 1991). The second category comprised private commercial radio stations that began to be launched in 1994 in Senegal and a few years later in Benin and Togo (PANOS 1993). The third category, private television stations, began broadcasting in the first decade of the 2000s (PANOS 2008).

The birth of these private media spelled a true media revolution for the people. Indeed from 1960 to 1990 there was only one radio station, one television station, and one newspaper in Benin and in Togo, all under government control. Only the government of Senegal authorized the creation of a political press run by opposition parties in addition to the creation of a handful of so-called independent publications alongside the state-controlled media. However, in reality these press organs were kept on a tight leash (Paye 1992).

Born in national contexts marked by a strong desire for change on the part of the people, the private media did not remain indifferent to public calls for democracy. In keeping with these aspirations, reporters working for private media have striven unceasingly in a number of different registers. Despite their limitations and contradictions, which we will address in further detail later on, they have acted as relays of public protest, taking strong stands in favour of democratic change and denouncing government corruption and various forms of human-rights violations.

Our goal here is to take stock of the relationship between the private media and social movements with a view to identifying their achievements, limitations. and future prospects. We will do so using a chronological approach. We will begin by addressing the pioneering role of the private print media in the democratization processes unfolding in Benin, Senegal, and Togo in the 1980s and 1990s. We will then focus on the role of independent radio stations and finally the new private television stations in these same processes.

Media Coverage: A Dominant Role in Social Change

As we have pointed out above, private newspapers began to emerge in the 1980s and 1990s when Benin, Senegal, and Togo were experiencing a profound crisis revolving around the key issue of the political, economic, social, and moral futures of the countries. In Benin and Togo, where private newspapers developed in an environment fraught with intense political upheaval punctuated by bloody events, the public's attention was focused on the upcoming national conferences, which were held up as a way out of the political dictatorships in power, against a backdrop of very real uncertainties as to whether change was truly possible. The Kérékou regime, under pressure from the people on the street, had agreed to the idea of organizing a national conference and a transition period (March 1990 to April 1991) as a prelude to the organization of multiparty presidential and legislative elections (Noudjenoume 1999). However, there was a likelihood that it would go back on its word to regain control of the situation. During the national conference of February 1990, Colonel Azonhiho and a handful of other officers from the Beninese army suggested at the time that the conference-goers should be arrested to save the regime. It seemed to them that the operation was possible since all the opponents and enemies of the regime were gathered in one spot (Hotel PLM-Alédjo in Cotonou).

In Togo the dismantling of all transitional democratic institutions and the assassination of radical opponents between 1990 and 1993 clearly demonstrated the firm will of General Eyadéma's regime not to give ground to popular uprisings. In Senegal private newspapers emerged in the electric preelectoral environment of 1988, when the political future of the country hung in the balance. In an ongoing power struggle between the ruling Socialist Party (PS) and its political opponents, the latter accused the former of preparing to manipulate the ballot once again.

The heads of state in all three countries seemed to assume a right to lifelong power despite their apparent lack of democratic legitimacy. Their ministers served record-beating terms, and cabinet shuffles merely meant portfolios were traded despite the political, economic, and social failures of the regimes in power.

Thus in all three countries, the end of the de facto or de jure single-party system and the issue of democratic change of government were core concerns for the people, who desperately wished to replace the elites in power. In addition to a context of political crisis with uncertain outcomes, the countries faced the failure of major state companies and banks. Under the structural adjustment programmes (SAPs) imposed by the International Monetary Fund (IMF) and the World Bank throughout the 1980s, these institutions made their partial or total liquidations conditions for financial support for economic recovery in all three countries. This generally resulted in numerous layoff plans affecting the futures of several thousand families. Private newspapers, developing in these troubled national contexts, immediately set themselves up as whistle-blowers, denouncing the authorities in power to promote the advent of democracy and the rule of law.

In Benin this whistle-blowing focused on practices of spoliation under the pseudo-Marxist regime (1972–1991) including practices that ruined all of the state banks—Banque Commerciale du Bénin (BCB), Banque Béninoise de Développement (BBD), and Caisse Nationale de Crédit Agricole (CNCA)[1]— and the country's public and semi-public corporations toward the end of the 1980s, causing the loss of thousands of jobs (Chabi 1993). Through a far-reaching whistle-blowing campaign, the private newspapers of Benin made an enormous contribution to the fall of Kérékou in 1991.

In Togo, where the democratic process was sullied by numerous human-rights violations particularly between 1990 and 1993, early editions of private newspapers denounced acts of violence by the army against demonstrators, opposition leaders, and members of democratic transition institutions. Senegal's private newspapers also acted as whistle-blowers. *Sud Hebdo, Wal Fadjri,* and *Le Cafard*

---

1 In 1989 total loans by these three banks to the Beninese economy amounted to CFA francs 149 billion: CFA francs 96.6 billion owing to BCB, CFA francs 35.6 billion to BBD, and CFA francs 18.8 billion to CNCA. Out of all those loans, only CFA francs 23.5 billion were considered sound. The remaining loans were considered recoverable doubtful debts (CFA francs 11.1 billion) or unrecoverable doubtful debts (CFA francs 113.4 billion). In terms of the latter, the public sector ended up with 62.4 billion (55 percent) in unpaid loans while the rest fell on the private sector (45 percent). BCB alone was saddled with CFA francs 93.6 billion in unrecoverable doubtful debts. In addition, in the space of five years, the bank lost forty-two times its capital of CFA francs 30 million, with 72,916 debtors who failed to pay off their accounts (Noudjenoume 1999, 41–42).

Libéré were actively committed to shedding light on the crisis in the Senegalese banking system at the end of the 1980s by publicly revealing the involvement of the authorities' clientelistic networks in their failure. They also mobilized alongside the opposition and civil society to denounce the electoral frauds witnessed during the presidential and legislative elections of February 1988.

During this period whistle-blowing actions against the established authorities by the private written press in Benin, Senegal, and Togo were highly innovative compared to the model of state journalism. The tremendous scope of the crisis affecting state-owned corporations and banks at the end of the 1980s, which the new private media helped to reveal, showed that the corruption and mismanagement that undermined these structures had been in existence for some time. It also illustrated that investigations to pinpoint practices of embezzlement and poor management were not core concerns of the state-run media.

In this context state journalists mentioned the crisis only a few times and only after it was made common knowledge by the closing of the state corporations and banks. However, as J. Barrat (1992) pointed out, state journalists downplayed the responsibility of the governments in power and their clientele in the economic and banking debacle, blaming the problems solely on a difficult international situation (including falling prices on raw materials prices on the international market run by the exploitative West) or accusing drought or cricket invasions. In Senegal these latter explanations were particularly common since the 1980s were effectively marked by both phenomena. In sum, according to the state media, the source of the crisis was either exogenous or ecological but in no case linked to the way in which the state apparatus had been managed for decades.

By pinpointing the responsibility of the elite in power in the state crisis of the late 1980s in Senegal, Benin, and Togo, private newspapers contributed to the emergence of social criticism of structural adjustment plans. They clearly informed the people that the implementation of those programmes and their negative fallout (budget cuts in health and education, layoffs, etc.) resulted from poor management on the parts of the governments in power and that the people should not have to pay in place of their leaders.

Throughout the 1980s and 1990s, the private print media also imposed itself as a genuine public forum open to all. Indeed under the single-party systems in force in Benin and Togo, and to a lesser extent under the dominant party in Senegal, only the dignitaries of the regime had the right to speak in public. Thus it was through private newspapers that opposition parties, trade unions, teachers, and students were able to express opinions in dissonance with the official stance on the crisis.

This democratic positioning of the private print media, embodied by pioneering newspapers such as *Tam-Tam Express*, *Le Forum de la Semaine*, and *Gazette du Golfe* in Benin; *Sud Hebdo* (which later became *Sud Quotidien*), *Wal Fadjri*, and *Le Cafard Libéré* in Senegal; and *Kpakpa Désenchanté* in Togo made these media enormously popular with the public. The private-press organs founded subsequently in Benin, Senegal, and Togo have continued to embody democratic coverage despite their contradictions.

The Contributions of Private Audiovisual Media

Calls for democratic change were amplified with the launch of private radio stations in the mid-1990s in Senegal and at the end of that decade in Benin and Togo. Because they used local languages, they gave the majority of the population, who were unable to read print media due to high illiteracy rates, direct access to local and national news picked up from private newspapers through press reviews or produced by private radio stations and dispensed in a tone of criticism toward the regimes in power, which the stations castigated for their inability to bring solutions to the pervading economic and social issues. The use of local languages also allowed the illiterate majority to participate in societal debates through interactive programmes such as "*Waax Sa Xalat*" on Senegalese private radio Sud FM (the title, in the Wolof language, means to speak one's mind; the programme gave listeners opportunities to air their views on political, economic, social, religious, and other subjects). Private radio stations also made decisive contributions to the broadening of the public space, a process already set in motion by private newspapers in Benin, Senegal, and Togo.

The recent launching of private national television stations was part of the dynamics echoing popular calls for greater democracy and democratic management of public funds. Because their unique technology combined sound and images, private television stations soon revealed themselves as formidable tools of information, striking fear into the hearts of the established authorities. This was demonstrated in Senegal, for one instance, when the regime of former head of state Abdoulaye Wade hesitated lengthily to grant licences to private television station promoters, fearing the damage that might be done to the image of the President or his government.

The Private Media: Central to the Development of Civic Consciousness

In light of the developments described above, the contributions of Benin's, Senegal's and Togo's private media to the democratization process and the people's aspirations for change can be summarized as follows:

- A culture of transparency in government management of public assets, in contrast with the opacity that characterized the Beninese, Senegalese, and Togolese states under the state media monopoly.
- A culture of accountability—i.e., obliging states to account for their management to the people, who are increasingly demanding and aware of their rights.
- An eye on the fairness and transparency of the presidential and legislative elections organized in recent years in Benin, Senegal, and Togo.
- Alternative platforms echoing popular protests and uprisings; prior to the existence of private media, state media did not report such actions.

When all is said and done, we can say private media, through their key roles as checks and balances, whistle-blowers, spaces for alternative debates, etc. have been for many years now at the heart of the development of a new consciousness. If people increasingly rise up against all forms of injustice perpetrated by their governments, it is because they are more aware of their rights thanks to the efforts of the private media.

Limitations of the Private Media

Generally speaking, despite the democratic role we have mentioned above, private media enterprises in Benin, Togo, and Senegal have great difficulty establishing themselves as economically and financially profitable businesses. The incomes they generate barely cover their overhead, and many reporters are not paid salaries. In addition to the limited circulation typical of private print media, virtually all private media enterprises in all sectors suffer from the small size of the advertising market.

In seeking a better understanding of the economic and financial difficulties affecting the private media, it would not be inaccurate to point to their inability to organize as real media enterprises with qualified commercial and human-resources departments equipped with clear strategic visions.

The economic and financial hardships besetting private media enterprises put many journalists at risk of a certain practice for which they criticize the elite in power: corruption. Many reporters, faced with unpaid or irregularly paid salaries, accept bribes to choose certain angles in their treatments of the news. On a broader scale some media owners are also affected by these practices of corruption.

In addition to the economic aspect, there is the issue of training. Most private media journalists in Benin, Senegal, and Togo cruelly lack training as they have not attended journalism school. On-the-job training is the general rule. Certainly there are some who truly believe in their work and manage to develop into professional journalists who are respected by their peers and the general public. But there are others whose professional practices are marked by amateurism, unreliable sources, and libel suits. Furthermore experience has shown that a lack of training often entails a failure to develop ingrained ethical reflexes against attempted corruption.

Future Prospects

In light of the importance of their democratic roles and the limitations we have identified, the private media in Benin, Senegal, and Togo need real media-enterprise management capacity-building programmes to ensure their economic and financial viability. These programmes, whose contents remain to be defined, could take the form of the creation of modular training cycles offered through media-monitoring workshops or seminars.

The programmes would target media owners and people who act as managers in the media without having the necessary skills base. They could also take place in the framework of long training cycles such as bachelor's or master's degrees in media enterprise management. In this case state or private journalism schools could create partnerships.

In Senegal, for instance, the communications departments of UFR-CRAC (Training and Research Unit—Civilizations, Religions, Arts, and Communications) at Gaston Berger University, CESTI (Centre for Information Science and Technology Studies), and ISSIC (Higher Institute of Information and Communications Sciences) could be partners. Scholarships for capacity building in media enterprise management could also be granted to media that have played proven roles in terms of democracy, credibility, and independence.

Given the lack of training affecting many journalists, there is a need to pursue the initiatives that have already been rolled out in this area by encouraging the development of both short and long training programmes: the short cycle could take the form of training seminars and workshops while the long cycle could take the form of degree-earning training leading to a *brevet de technicien supérieur* ("advanced technical certificate") or a bachelor's or master's in the most innovative areas of journalism, especially those linked to information and communications technologies. In this framework partnerships could be created with existing training structures.

In Senegal efforts have been made but remain insufficient. SYNPICS (the union of information and communications professionals of Senegal) has been able to secure only 10 percent of state aid to the media—in the area of CFA francs 300 million on average since 1996—for training. However, this amount is not enough to cover training needs. Furthermore the regularity with which the aid is actually paid out depends on the goodwill of the powers that be. Similarly it is important to decentralize capacity building for journalists. To take the case of Senegal once again, training takes place mainly in Dakar, yet there is a real need for training in the regions outside the capital. Most regional correspondents lack training in journalism.

The Convention of Young Reporters makes efforts, but these alone are not enough. Whenever there is a major event on the national political agenda, such as a presidential election or legislative elections, journalist-monitoring programmes should be multiplied to ensure journalists understand the issues at stake and can explain them to the people. Initiatives do exist in this area, but they need to be reinforced.

Conclusion

If African people today use a variety of means to express their discontent and frustration with the political, economic, and social problems besetting them, it is because they have developed a stronger civic consciousness and honed their critical skills. The independent private media have played and continue to play major roles in this process of heightened awareness and the maturing of the civic consciousness. Since their advent they have tirelessly contributed to the birth of a new political culture that has progressively distanced itself from the spirit of resignation that has long characterized African populations in the face of authoritarian abuses perpetrated by their governments. Thanks to the actions of the private media, the people are more aware that the authorities in power must be held to account for their management of public affairs.

Also thanks to the actions of the private media, people have become aware that they hold the power to sanction through presidential or legislative elections any authorities that do not produce the desired results. The changes of government in Benin in 1991, 1996, and 2001 and in Senegal in 2000 and 2012 are good examples of this power to sanction triggered by the private media. Based on the examples we have seen in Benin, Senegal, and Togo, it is safe to say that with a little bit of professional and ethical fine tuning, Africa's private media can be credible actors in the processes of social change on the continent.

References

Akindes, F. 1995. *Les Mirages de la démocratie en Afrique subsaharienne francophone.* Dakar: Codesria.

Barrat, J. 1992. *Géographie économique des médias: Médias et Développement.* Paris: Litec.

Chabi, M. 1993. *Banqueroute—Mode d'emploi (un marabout dans les grilles de la maffia béninoise).* Porto Novo: Éditions Gazette Livres.

Conac, G. 1993. "Les processus de démocratisation en Afrique" in G. Conac, ed. *L'Afrique en transition vers le pluralisme politique.* Paris: Economica.

Diop, M. C. and Diouf, M. 1990. *Le Sénégal sous Abdou Diouf. État et Société.* Paris: Karthala.

Diop, S. J. 2001. "Les élections au Sénégal, de l'indépendance à la fin des années 1990" in *Médias et élections au Sénégal : la presse et les nouvelles technologies de l'information dans le processus électoral.* Dakar, PANOS. 2001.

Faye, M. 2008. *Presse privée écrite en Afrique francophone: enjeux démocratiques.* Paris: L'Harmattan.

Frère, M.-S. "Dix ans de pluralisme en Afrique francophone." *Les Cahiers du Journalisme* 9 (2001): 28–59.

Frère, M.-S. 2000. *Presse et Démocratie en Afrique—Les mots et les maux de la transition.* Paris: Karthala.

Frère, M.-S. "Démocratie au Bénin et au Niger." *Mots. Les langages du politique* 59 (1999): 89–104.

Gaba, L. 2000. *L'État de Droit et le développement économique en Afrique subsaharienne*. Paris: L'Harmattan.

Loum, N. 2003. *Les médias et l'État au Sénégal—L'impossible autonomie*. Paris: L'Harmattan.

Noudjenoume, P. 1999. *La démocratie au Bénin—Bilan et perspectives*. Paris: L'Harmattan.

PANOS/UJAO. 1993. *Le pluralisme radiophonique en Afrique de l'Ouest*. Paris: L'Harmattan.

PANOS/UJAO/SEP. 1991. *Presse francophone d'Afrique: vers le pluralisme*. Paris: L'Harmattan.

Paye, M. 1992. "La presse et le pouvoir" in M.C. Diop, ed. *Sénégal: Trajectoires d'un État*. Paris: Karthala.

Perret, T. "Le journaliste africain face à son statut." *Les Cahiers du Journalisme* 9 (2001): 154–169.

Toulabor, C.M. 1986. *Le Togo sous Eyadéma*. Paris: Karthala.

Tudesq, A.-J. 1995. *Feuilles d'Afrique—Etude de la presse de l'Afrique subsaharienne*. Paris, Maison des Sciences de l'Homme d'Aquitaine.

www.ingramcontent.com/pod-product-compliance
Lightning Source LLC
Chambersburg PA
CBHW071041290526
45795CB00004B/1260